Published by PATMOS PRESS
917 Valencia Road, South Daytona, FL 32119
904 788-9386   FAX 904 788-0325

E-mail- info@patmospress.com
Website - www.patmospress.com

QUICK REFERENCE

A Note from the Author

While this Book is mainly based on the Manifestations of the three Weeping Icons of the Holy Mother and Ever-Virgin Mary on Long Island in 1960, I found it necessary at various points, when relating the Events pertaining to the *"Divine Signs,"* to interject pertinent historical teachings and descriptions of the Orthodox Christian Church. This will enable the non-Eastern Orthodox reader to acquire some basic knowledge to better comprehend, how these are intertwined with the subject at hand.

I think this is very important, because it will provide the reader with a foundation, or at least some background, to connect the 20th Century Icon Manifestations in this Book with pertinent historical linkages to the life of the Church, — throughout Her two thousand year history.

(To understand the terms of the Greek Orthodox Church, please refer to the Glossary on page 195).

Why did She Cry?

✳

An eye-witness account
of the Manifestations
of the
3 Weeping Icons of the "Panagia"
as they happened within the boundaries
of the
St. Paul's Greek Orthodox Parish
Hempstead, New York

March 16, 1960
April 12, 1960
May 7, 1960

by
Fr. George Papadeas

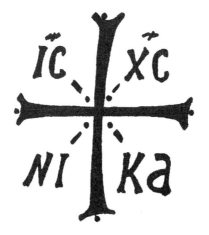

"IC" **"XC"** These four letters have a slur on top, according to a practice of the Byzantine Iconographers. (see p. 138) They painted only the first and last letter of a name omitting the letters in between. For example, **"IC"** is Jesus and **"XC"** is Christ. The word **"NIKA"** means "conquers." Thus: **"Jesus Christ conquers."**

Year 2000 ~ The 40th Anniversary
of the three Holy Icons of the "Weeping Madonna."

Dedication

Offered as a gift of love,
adoration and gratitude
to the Giver of all Gifts,
our Father in Heaven.

Also to His faithful children
Peter and Pagona Catsounis, whose
Icon is enshrined in the St. Paul's Cathedral.

And no less, to my wife Bess, and
our children, for their invaluable
assistance to publish this Book.

September, 2000

Preface

The number 40 is associated with great Events mentioned in the Holy Scriptures, as well as in the Eastern Orthodox traditions. For example, the Orthodox Christians associate this number with the 40 day Fast for the Advent Period, and the Great Fast of 40 days preceding Holy Week.

We remember from the Old Testament that Moses received the 10 Commandments on Mount Sinai after having fasted for 40 days. (Exodus 34:28).

From the New Testament we learn that before our Lord Jesus Christ commenced His earthly Ministry, He had fasted for 40 days and nights in the wilderness. There, He was tempted by Satan three times. It was at this time that He uttered a saying, which should be a vivid reminder for all Christians: **"Man shall not live by bread alone, but by every word that proceeds from the mouth of God."** (Matthew 4:2-4)

We also know, that after the Lord's Glorious Resurrection, He appeared to His Disciples and the outer group for 40 days. On the 40th day, the Lord with all His devoted followers had gathered together on a mound just outside Jerusalem. Standing on this mound He blessed them, and suddenly, to their surprise, they were stricken with awe seeing Him ascending into Heaven. (Luke 24:50-51).

In Luke 2:25-32, we read of the Jewish tradition of mothers bringing their infants to the Temple to be blessed on the 40th day of their birth. Revering this Judaistic tradition, the *All-Holy Mother, St. Mary* had brought the infant Jesus to the awaiting Prophet Simeon at the Temple to be blessed.

Simeon had constantly been praying for the Lord to grant him sufficient years, in the hope that he could personally witness the Messiah's coming to earth. His prayer was answered. Receiving the Infant Jesus in his arms, he blessed the Name of God and said:

"Now Lord, let Your servant depart in peace according to Your word; for my eyes have seen Your salvation, which You have prepared in the presence for all people; a Light of revelation to the Gentiles, and the glory of Your People Israel."

This Biblical Event is still traditionally practiced only in the Orthodox Church from ancient times until today, and will continue for all time. On the 40th day, the mother brings her infant to Church to be blessed by the Priest of her Parish.

From the Sanctuary, the Priest proceeds to the Narthex where the mother awaits with her infant. After pertinent prayers, the Priest blesses and receives the infant from the mother, as Simeon had received the Infant Jesus. Proceeding down aisle of the Nave he says three times:

"I shall enter Your House, and I shall worship in Your Sacred Temple." and, "The servant of God is churched in the Name of the Father and of the Son and of the Holy Spirit."

Standing before the Holy Altar, and raising the infant in an offering position, the Priest repeats the identical words of the Prophet Simeon when he had received the Infant Jesus in the Temple of Jerusalem.

It is now, in the year 2000, that I hinge and connect onto the *"religious number, 40!"*

After 40 years, I come to relive and record the Manifestations and Events of the three Holy Icons, as they did happen in the homes of two of my parishioners of St. Paul's Greek Orthodox Cathedral in Hempstead, Long Island, where I was the Pastor.

For many years I had contemplated writing this Book. But somehow, — for perhaps unjustifiable reasons, — I delayed doing so until the present.

I do believe, however, that not all postponements are in vain! Even though 40 years have lapsed into history, the Events of the Weeping Madonnas, as the Holy Icons have been labeled, are very much alive in the hearts and minds of many of my former parishioners and friends, with whom I have not lost contact, even though I have been away from my beloved St. Paul's Parish since 1963.

I believe that this book will serve as a revival of sorts to the countless souls, who hold so very dear their love for the Lord and His *"All-Holy Mother"* — the protecting and loving Mother of us all — the *"All-Holy Ever-Virgin Mary."*

For those who did not witness these *Manifestations,* this Book will hopefully serve to fortify their faith, that God is always with us, and at times extends His Merciful Hand to bring His supernatural acts before us for our edification.

St. John the Evangelist, in the last part of his Gospel, relating his testimony of the things that the Lord Jesus said and did, states: **"This is the Disciple, who bears witness of these things, and wrote these things, and we know that his witness is true."** (John 21:24)

Humbly, and unworthy though I may be, — I take the liberty to paraphrase this 24th verse of the 21st Chapter of the Evangelist St. John's Gospel by applying it to my effort and stating, that **"I bore witness to the *Manifestations* of the three Holy Icons of our All-Holy Mother, which shed tears, and am now writing these things, and I know that my witness is true."**

Fr. George Papadeas

God works His Wonders through People, always for Supreme Purposes

Before commencing to write about the wondrous *Signs* of the Lord, I bring to you some passages from the Gospel of St. Luke referring to the *"All-Holy Theotokos"* (Greek, for "Birth-Giver of God"), the central Person of this Book.

Our Holy Mother St. Mary is referred in this Book as a prime example of obedience to the will of God. When The Archangel Gabriel stated to Her, *"The Holy Spirit will come upon you, and the power of the Most High will overshadow you; therefore, the Child to be born of You will be called Holy, the Son of God,"* Mary humbly replied: **"Behold, I am the handmaid of the Lord; let it be to me according to Your word."** (Luke 1:35,38).

Submission to the will of God was always primary in Her life. That is why Elizabeth, the mother of St. John the Baptist, said to St. Mary when she went to visit her: *"Blessed are You among women, and blessed is the Fruit of Your womb."* (Luke 1:42).

Also, It was during this visit that Her relative Elizabeth, who was with child, prophetically said to her:

"Why is this granted to me, that the Mother of my Lord should come to me? For behold, when the voice of your greeting came to my ears, the babe in my womb leaped for joy. And blessed is she, who believed that there would be a fulfillment of what was spoken to her from the Lord." (Luke 1:43-45).

I also bring to you verses 46-55 from the lst Chapter of St. Luke's Gospel. I chose this excerpt, in order to show you the magnitude of the soul of this chosen young Maiden from Nazareth. Blessed by the Holy Spirit, as seen in the verses below, she exclaimed Her submission and profound gratitude to the Lord with elements of prophecy.

And Mary said: (Luke, verses 46-55)

(Also known as the *Magnificat!*)

"My soul magnifies the Lord, and my spirit rejoices in God my Saviour,

for He has regarded the low estate of his handmaiden.

For behold, henceforth all generations will call me blessed;

for He who is Mighty has done great things for me, and Holy is His Name.

And His mercy is on those who fear Him, from generation to generation.

He has shown strength in His arm; He has scattered the proud in the imagination of their hearts,

He has brought down the mighty from their thrones, and exalted the humble;

He has filled the hungry with good things, and the rich he has sent away empty.

He has helped His servant Israel, in remembrance of His mercy, as He spoke to our fathers, Abraham and to his posterity forever!"

❂   ❂   ❂

A Word about the Holy Orthodox Church

Before I commence to describe the Events surrounding the three Icons, I deem it necessary to give a brief historical account of the Holy Orthodox Church and the veneration of the Icons, as revered in the Eastern Orthodox Church.

Much to the sorrow of the Church, the great Schism of 1054 A.D. split the Church of Christ into two large Bodies, as both of these exist today. One is the Western, Latin, Roman Catholic, or Papal Church, and the other is the Eastern Orthodox Catholic Church. Until 1054 A.D. Christ's Church was one Body, with five totally distinct and independent Centers, as had been crystallized from the earliest years.

These were governed independently by their respective Bishops, — all equal in authority, — and most importantly with an identity in common regarding the Faith. They were in Jerusalem, Antioch in Syria (today in Damascus), Rome, Alexandria in Egypt and Constantinople.

Since the Bishop of Rome was in the Capital of the vast Roman Empire, he was given a title of honor by the other four Bishops. They honored him with the title *"Primus inter Pares."* (Latin, for *"first among equals"*). However, in no way did this honorary title give the Bishop of Rome any authority over his other four Brothers in Christ, except perhaps to preside at any Meetings.

This *"primacy"* of honor, or distinction, perhaps can be somewhat understood by our experience in today's world with a comparable example. The Roman Catholic Cardinal of New York seems to have a kind of pre-eminence among the other Cardinals of our Country.

However, by no means is he superior to any other Cardinal, but the fact that his See is in New York City, the most prominent City of America, and of all the world, the New York Cardinal is, as we say, more in the limelight.

Since July 20, 1054 A.D., the saddest Day in the history of the Christian Church, the Western part of Christianity has been under the jurisdiction of the Bishop of Rome.

The Eastern part of the Christian Church was comprised of the Churches of Jerusalem, Antioch, Alexandria and Constantinople. Until today, these Centers continue to be completely unified in Faith as **"the One, Holy, Catholic and Apostolic Church,"** from the Apostolic times. In recent centuries, the head Prelates of the Balkan Orthodox Countries and beyond have become autocephalous with the blessings of the Ecumenical Patriarchate in Constantinople. The totality of all these Orthodox Churches are a completely unified Church in Faith.

They have remained independent of one another jurisdictionally, as they have been from the Apostolic times, but unified as one Orthodox entity. This is consonant with the spirit of the Ancient Church; *"Unity in diversity!"* These four Centers of Ancient Christendom, came to be known as Patriarchates, each headed by a Patriarch. Collectively they comprise the Eastern Orthodox Church in full communion until today, as they have been from the initial Apostolic years of Christianity.

The term **"catholic"** is a Greek adjective meaning **"universal."** It is part of the official designation of the Eastern Orthodox Church, but the term *"Catholic"* is not commonly used by the Eastern Orthodox Catholic Church, except in official documents or declarations, and in the Nicene-Constantinopolitan Creed.

During the first eight centuries the undivided Church convened in seven Ecumenical Councils to limit the danger of the heresies. These Councils defined the Dogmas of the Church, and that of Canon Law, based on the teachings of the Bible, the life, the tradition and the history of the Church.

There was full participation of all the five Centers of the undivided Christendom in these seven Ecumenical Councils of the first 8 Centuries.

The faithful adherence to the Dogmas, as defined and promulgated by the Ecumenical Councils has constituted the Orthodox Church's vital link with the Ancient Christian Church, and is the reason that there have never been any disputes, or divisions, or any need for reforms in the Eastern Orthodox Church.

The Nicene Creed, recited in both the Eastern and Western Church during the Liturgies is a product of the first two Ecumenical Councils. It is interesting here to note, that all of the seven Ecumenical Councils were held in the Eastern territory of undivided Christianity and specifically in and around Constantinople.

The first Ecumenical Council was held in Nicaea of Asia Minor (near Constantinople) in the year 325 A.D. This Council gave us the first seven Articles of the Creed. The second Ecumenical Council was convened in Constantinople in 381 A.D. and completed the Creed with the last 5 Articles, for a total of 12. This very Creed, after a history of over 1600 years, is repeated in its original text, as bequeathed to us, in all the Divine Liturgies of the Orthodox Churches, as well as in other Orthodox Services, word for word, as it was dogmatized.

The ninth Article of the Nicene-Constantinopolitan Creed specifies: (I believe) **"in One, Holy, Catholic and Apostolic Church."**

This definition is most important, because it specifies the **four vital attributes of the Church,** which are fundamental to the validity and life of the Church. These attributes are directly linked to our Lord and Saviour Jesus Christ, through His Holy Apostles.

In this article, the Creed firstly specifies that the Church is **"One."** It is one, because the Lord instituted only one Church through His Holy Apostles, who were commissioned to preach the Gospel to the Nations.

Their unified message of salvation brought into being the formal Church, which Christ instituted, as an historical reality, and therefore was to continue as one Church for all ages to come.

Unfortunately, as mentioned, this unity was severed with the lamented Schism of the Western or Papal Church from the Eastern on that fateful day of July 20, 1054 A.D. It is the prayer, offered in every Divine Liturgy and all other Prayer Services of the Holy Orthodox Church, that once again the Church will be completely re-united, based on the history and experience of the first eleven Centuries.

Secondly, the Church, as stated in the 9th Article of the Creed is **"Holy,"** because our Lord and Saviour is Holy. Next, the Church is also **"Catholic,"** (Greek word for "Universal") because the Lord consecrated and commissioned only His Holy Apostles to preach the Gospel to all Nations and continue same by consecrations and ordinations, thereby instituting the historic Church.

Lastly, the Church is **"Apostolic,"** because the Lord's Disciples were the consecrated Apostles. They were consecrated as the first Bishops of the Church by the Lord Jesus Himself on the same Day of His glorious Resurrection from the dead. Although the Lord also had an outer circle of devoted followers, He chose to consecrate and exclusively commission only His Holy Apostles to found the Church. (Matthew 28:19). As is known from the Scriptures, Judas Iscariot, who betrayed the Lord was replaced by Matthias, who became the twelfth Apostle.

When the Lord miraculously appeared before His Apostles on the first Day of His Resurrection, even though the doors of the Upper Room were secured because of fear for their lives, His greeting was: **"Peace be with you; as the Father has sent Me, I also send you."**

And when He had said this, He breathed on them, and said to them, **"Receive the Holy Spirit. If you forgive the sins of any, their sins shall be forgiven them; if you retain the sins of any, they shall be retained."** (John 20:21-23).

The fourth attribute of the Church, **"Apostolic,"** is what the Church historically believes and teaches as *"Apostolic Succession."* This gives the Church the authenticity, as it was first given by the Lord only to His Apostles. It is this Apostolic Succession which gives validity to the Church, through the unbroken links in the chain of the successive Consecrations and Ordinations from the Day of the Pentecost until the present, and surely for all ages to come.

For example, I am a Priest of the Greek Orthodox Church. I was ordained by the Bishop of New England Athenagoras Kavadas, at the St. George Greek Orthodox Church in Springfield, Massachusetts on the Holy Day of the Annunciation of the Virgin Mary, March 25, 1942.

The Bishop who ordained me, was himself previously consecrated a Bishop by three other Canonical Bishops. They, in turn, had been consecrated by other Canonical Bishops and so on. Each ordination, or consecration, constitutes a vital link to the unbroken chain, which historically connects the present day Orthodox Priesthood to one of the Holy Apostles, and surely to the Founder of the Church, our Lord and Saviour Jesus Christ.

Here in America the Greek Orthodox Church receives Her authority from the Ecumenical Patriarch in Constantinople, who in direct lineage is the successor of the first-called to the Apostles, St. Andrew.

The Lord chose, as has been mentioned, to consecrate only his Holy Apostles to found His Church, having given them the authority to perpetuate the life of the Church through Consecrations and Ordinations. Thus, the Apostles were the first link in the chain linking them with Christ.

Their successors were directly linked to them to form the second link and so on. Continuing to add links down through the ages until the present day with the unbroken linkage in the chain is known as **"Apostolic Succession,"** as was affirmed and dogmatized in the 9th article of the Nicene-Constantinopolitan Creed.

Also, in variance to those who campaign for the ordination of women, the answer was given by the Lord Himself. While he had scores of faithful followers, men and women, He chose to consecrate only the twelve Apostles! During the time that the Apostles preaching practically all over the then known world, this did not change. We see that St. Paul also had dedicated men and women followers, who were a vital part of the Church tending to Church matters, while he was in different cities preaching, baptizing and instituting the Parish Churches.

St. Paul's missionary work of establishing Churches was a successful ongoing process. When he first stepped on European ground, his first act was to baptize the first woman of Europe named Lydia. Throughout his unique missionary endeavors, St. Paul, although assisted in his mission by women, had never made any mention, nor even hinted of perhaps ordaining women.

Without a doubt, the Lord and His Apostles knew and appreciated greatly the importance of women to the call of the Church. Their importance has never waned, and is very vital and very much alive in Her history down through the ages, as it will always be.

Even from the days of the New Testament it is specifically noted, that the women were the last to leave from the scene of the Cross, and the first to arrive at the Tomb to proclaim the Resurrection of the Lord!

From the early Centuries of Christianity we see the Church summoning devoted women and tonsuring them as Nuns in the Monasteries. Their role in the Church is distinctive and positive, and has remained so until the present day. The role of women was always important in the life of the Church, but was never in the realm for them of being ordained into the Holy Priesthood.

Would not the Lord, whose works were all complete and perfect, have included women in the college of the 12 Apostles since He had the wisdom and the absolute power to do so?

Could anyone ever think, or even conceive, that the Lord would have made such an omission, or that He hadn't completed His mission? That is why it is difficult to understand how such liberty and license has been taken in these last few years by some *"progressive Clergymen"* of various Denominations to fill in the *"gaps,"* as it were, that were supposedly left open by the Lord!

Surely, we can never for a moment even conceive of the Lord omitting, or falling short on any plan, or leaving a supposed gap! Especially one, that dealt with His Church, which as St Paul states: **"that He (Christ) might present it to Himself a glorious Church, not having spot, or wrinkle, or any such thing; but that it should be holy and without blemish!"** (Ephesians 5:27).

❊   ❊   ❊

The Holy Icons in relation to the Byzantine Architecture and in Orthodox Life

In the Orthodox world, down through the ages, *"Miracles"* and *"Divine Signs"* have been experienced through Holy Icons. I don't know, if previously to the

Manifestations on Long Island there had been a similar or comparable *Manifestation* in America. I sincerely doubt this, because if there was, I believe that the battery of New York Reporters, who had thoroughly covered these Manifestations, day after day for months, would have discovered some clue during their investigation and would have reported accordingly.

One of the expressions which the Orthodox Church has in common with the Western or Papal Church, is our profound reverence for the Person of our *"All-Holy Mother"* and *"Ever-Virgin Mary."* In both Churches, there are many meaningful and inspiring Services dedicated in Her honor.

In the Eastern Orthodox Church particularly, the Services are numerous and the Iconography most prolific, regarding the portrayals of the *"All-Holy Theotokos."*

There are so many different Icons painted of the Holy Mother, — portraying Her alone, or holding the Christ Child. The Roman Catholic Church early on had introduced statues in Her Churches, along with Icons that had existed.

However, the Western Church's Iconography differs in art-form from the Eastern. But, in recent years, we see more and more Icons in Roman Catholic Bookstores of the Ever-Virgin Mary, reproductions of the originals from parts of Greece, Constantinople and Russia, exemplifying the traditional Byzantine Iconography.

The marked difference from Eastern Iconography, when one views Western Religious art is, that the Icons of the Western tradition appear to be more anthropomorphic, whereas the Byzantines in the East sought to project the spiritual, rather than the physical. That is why in the Byzantine Iconography, the portrayals appear so austere in their expression. The disproportions of the physical were always intentional, in order to emphasize the spiritual.

Regarding the three Icons of the Holy Mother, which shed tears within the St. Paul's Cathedral Parish boundaries on Long Island, it was very interesting to note that of the three, the first tearing Icon *"Mother of sorrows"* was a product of Western Iconography, whereas the other two were products of traditional Byzantine Iconography.

Unfortunately, the millions of the Protestant Churches do not have Icons in their Churches. Perhaps in the strife and their final break with the Church of Rome early in the 16th Century, the Protestant Reformers sought to justify their actions with the Old Testament verses in (Exodus 20:4 and Leviticus 26:1) regarding *"graven images."*

However, even from the earliest traditions of the Christian Church, and especially in the Catacombs, we see religious paintings or Icons on the walls. These were visual portrayals, which helped to inspire the first Christians to endure the horrible persecutions of the first 300 years, and to keep them in sharper focus with the Lord and His Apostles.

It may be noted here, that the most notable Reformer Martin Luther, in all his years as a dynamic Dominican Priest faithfully serving the Church of Rome, never once had condemned using Icons or statues to adorn the Churches.

I think that it has been most appropriately stated, that Icons are **"Windows to Heaven."** Through the portrayals on Icons, one is readily brought into contact with the Holy Trinity, the Lord Jesus, the Ever Virgin Mother, the Holy Apostles and the countless Saints of the Church whom we should seek to emulate.

Simply expressed, an Icon should be considered as a junction of the Mystery of God and the reality of man.

I often wondered, when shopping at inter-denominational Religious Bookstores, I would notice people making purchases of crosses and lithographed prints of Jesus, as well as Biblical scenes. Why would they be purchasing Icons when they are not used in their Churches? I would conclude, that these lithographed prints were not merely to decorate walls in their home, but were hung by the faithful as items of inspiration, and to keep them in touch as it were, when they glanced at them.

In viewing these Icons or Prints, they could not but bring to mind the Lord and His mission upon this Earth!

What the Protestants then do for their homes, is what the Church had been doing from the earliest years down through the Ages, artistically decorating the wall space of all the Orthodox Churches. The Protestant Churches as mentioned, do not use Iconography in their Houses of Worship, even though their constituents have Icons at home.

Imagine if photography had existed during the time of our Lord, of His Apostles and of the Canonized Saints of the Church! Surely the aforementioned would have been photographed as Celebrities over and over. Had that been the case, would not their photographs have been displayed in Churches for the purpose of inspiring and uplifting Her Faithful, as well as in their homes?

Do we not carry photos of our loved ones in our wallets to keep them close to us? We surely never forget our loved ones, and at times when we journey afar, do we not pull out our wallet to look at the photos with much love and affection? Most often, we will even bring them to our lips and bestow upon them our loving kiss.

That is precisely the analogy of the Icons in the Orthodox Church, or in our home. In viewing the Icons, our mind is immediately put in touch with the relative portrayals of the Holy Figures, which remind us of their life and sacrifices. In the Orthodox Churches, there are very many Icons portraying the countless Saints and Martyrs of Christianity.

Had not these Martyrs persisted in their faith, which ultimately cost them their very life, especially during the first 300 years of the Roman persecutions, could the Church have ever survived? It is the blood of these Martyrs, in imitation of our Lord, that nurtured the newly planted *"Tree of Christianity,"* so that it firmly rooted even in the face of the many repeated horrible and indescribable persecutions.

We know that the Lord shed His innocent Blood as a ransom for many, to wash away the sins of mankind for all time!

The Holy Martyrs, completely dedicated to, and inspired by the Lord, very willingly sacrificed their life also, so that the Church would root and survive.

Their sacrifice for the Lord gained them their rightful place in Heaven. They are considered our elder Brothers and Sisters in Heaven. We pray to them asking for their intercessions to the Lord in our behalf. While the Saints are revered by the Church and Her faithful, **there is no question that worship belongs strictly and only to God.**

The Orthodox Christians do not worship the Saints. They simply revere them lovingly, and pray to them that they may intercede for us to God. The Saints were canonized by the Church for their saintly life, as well as having chosen to give their last measure for the Lord.

In the Eastern Orthodox tradition, the acceptance of Saints begins at the grass roots. The Church usually does not take the initiative to canonize the Saints. The Saints are primarily accepted as such in the conscience of the people, who had some direct or indirect experience with them. The facts of their saintly life very soon, or gradually spread after their death. Popular opinion was crystallized; their supreme Christian merits were widespread and fully accepted.

Usually, after having some miracle or sign associated with them, the Church steps forward to place Her seal of approval to proclaim them as Saints, to be revered by all their brothers and sisters here on earth, striving to find themselves on the path of salvation.

The Orthodox Christians pray to the Saints as their having found favor with God, to intercede for us.

This is clearly understood from St. James Epistle Chapter 5 Verse 1:

"The effectual fervent prayer of a righteous person availeth much!"

At Baptism, the Orthodox Christian Parents customarily name their child after a Saint, who then becomes its Patron Saint for life. The Orthodox celebrate their Nameday on the Anniversary Day of their Patron Saint.

However, we do come across Parents, who overlook this spiritual and uplifting legacy. Instead of selecting the name of a Saint for their child, they choose to name their child after one of the *"famous"* Hollywood stars, or after some *"popular"* personality of the entertainment world, regardless if their life may be questionable!

Most certainly, this denotes the remoteness of these Parents to the names and lives of the glorious Saints — the *"Stars" in the Heavenly Galaxy*, who could constitute true role models for their children.

"Windows to Heaven"

The Orthodox Icon is a *"written image."* Its subject matter can be read like a book. To the Orthodox Christians, the Icon is more than religious art; its role in Orthodox life is broader, than merely the visual portrayal of religious subjects.

In Colossians 1:16 St. Paul states that **"Christ is the image of the invisible God."**

The **"Windows to Heaven,"** — that is the Icons, offer us a place within the secular reality of our hectic daily routines to contemplate the spiritual reality of God's word, and its role in our lives.

Three considerations should be kept in mind regarding the Icons.

1. The use of Iconography has evolved from the very beginnings of Christianity in the Catacombs.

Established as an important element of the Church from the earliest times, and re-affirmed after the Iconoclastic Period at the Seventh Ecumenical Council in 787 A.D., the Byzantine art form flourished during the one thousand year span of the Byzantine Empire — until 1453 A.D, — the year that the Ottoman Turks overran and subjugated the Great Byzantine Empire.

Canonical forms of Byzantine art were implemented and passed from master to pupil with extreme care to accurately preserve the theological truths portrayed on the Icons.

Icons in the Orthodox Church.

The Orthodox Church Edifice is a cruciform, crowned at the center with a dome, symbolizing the universe filled with the presence of God, His Angels, and the Saints. Icons depicting these images follow a fixed placement pattern in the Orthodox Church.

Upon entering an Orthodox Church, one is immediately welcomed by the Icon of the *"Platytera"* (Greek, for "Broader than the Heavens") on the apse (semi-circular half dome in the Sanctuary) of the east wall of the Church.* Her arms are outstretched, as if to be welcoming us to give us a great big hug.

---

* — The Orthodox Churches by tradition face eastwardly, because the *"Light"* came from the East. The Holy Altar also faces eastwardly.

This Icon presents the *"Panagia"* (Greek, for *"All-Holy),"* with the young Jesus sitting on Her lap. Seeing the *"Platytera"* in the apse of the Sanctuary, we are reminded of the role of the *"Theotokos,"* — that She is truly the link between Heaven and Earth. She constitutes this link, as seen in the Orthodox Church, because the *"Pantocrator,"* (Greek, "holding all in His Hands") painted in the Dome, symbolizes the Lord looking down from Heaven; — the Faithful have their place in the Nave, — and the *"Platytera"* is the link in the middle, — between the Faithful in the Nave, and the *"Pantocrator"* at the highest point of the Church. The Iconography here gives us the theology of the stature of the *"Panagia,"* as being the link between Heaven and Earth.

On the outer arch of the apse of the *"Platytera,"* that is, on a semi-circular panel from one end of the Sanctuary to the other, arching like a rainbow we see the Holy Apostles.

Proceeding down the center aisle toward the *"Iconostasis"* and looking up toward the dome we see the majestic image of Christ, the *"Pantocrator."* Usually, around the base of the dome we see the great Prophets, who many hundreds of years before Christ had foretold all the Events of the Lord's life, as recorded in the Old Testament.

The dome is supported by four massive columns, connecting the Nave, the Transepts and the Sanctuary through four arches. These arches meet at the base of the dome forming a triangle above each column, called pendentives. On these four pendentives we usually see the Icons of the four Evangelists, Matthew, Mark, Luke and John.

Facing the Sanctuary we see the *"Iconostasis,"* (The Icon Screen, or wall. — Literally *"Icon stand")* separating the Nave from the Sanctuary. The Sanctuary is the *"Holy of Holies."* Only the ordained Clergy and the tonsured Altar Boys may enter the Sanctuary.

The *"Iconostasis"* has a high arch over the middle passage-way from the Nave to the Sanctuary known as the *"Orea Pili,"* ("Beautiful Archway, Gateway, or Royal Doors"). The Royal Doors, or Gates under this arch are always closed, except for any Service being held.

Behind the Royal Doors or Gates, is the Holy Altar in the center of the Sanctuary.

On the *"Iconostasis"* there are usually six Icons, as seen in all the Orthodox Churches, always in a standard position. To the right facing the Royal Gates we see the Icon of the Lord sitting on His Throne holding an open Bible. Next to the Lord we see the Icon of St. John the Baptist, the Forerunner of Christ.

Next to St. John is the Icon of the Archangel Gabriel. This Icon is positioned on the southern door of the *"Iconostasis,"* through which the Altar Boys re-enter the Sanctuary during Services. No one, except the Clergy may enter the Sanctuary through the Royal Gates *("Orea Pili").*

Facing the *"Iconostasis"* to the left of the Royal Gates we see the Icon of the *"All-Holy Mother"* holding the young Jesus. Next to the *"All-Holy Mother"* we see the Icon of the Saint or Saints, in whose honor the Church is named.

When viewing this Icon we immediately learn the Name of the particular Church we're in without having to inquire. Next to the Icon of the Church's Name is the northern door of the *"Iconostasis."* On this door we see the Icon of the Archangel Michael. Through this northern door the Clergy and the Altar Boys exit for all processions. Upon re-entering the Sanctuary in any Service, the Clergy proceed through the Royal Gates *("Orea Pili")* and the Altar Boys through the southern door.

Symbolically it is both these Archangels, Michael and Gabriel, portrayed on the northern and southern door of the *Iconostasis,* who guard the Sanctuary, as it were. These 6 Icons are standard on the *"Iconostasis."* Depending on the wall space available in the front areas of the Church on either side of the *"Iconostasis,"* other Icons, or Biblical presentations are seen.

Around the walls of the Sanctuary below the apse with the Icon of the *"Platytera,"* we usually see the great Doctors and Saints of the Church, the Three Hierarchs, St. Basil the Great, St. Gregory the Theologian, St. John the Chrysostom, as well as the Pillar of Orthodoxy, St. Athanasios the Great. All these luminaries of the Church lived in the 4th Century A.D.

On the walls of the Nave and Narthex we see Icons and Murals with portrayals of the Nativity, the Baptism of our Lord, the Holy Transfiguration, the Resurrection, the Pentecost, etc., all of which provide a visual presentation of theological teachings of the Church.

The many Icons in the Orthodox Church provide a warm and encompassing feeling for the worshipper. They serve to envelop a person into a religious sphere and frame of mind. Icons are an aid, which can help to bring about an elevation above the mundane, by participating in prayer during the Divine Liturgies and other Church Services.

2. The Icon is a teaching medium of the Church.

By viewing the Icons, the Faithful can reflect on the lives of the Saints and Martyrs as supreme examples of complete dedication and submission to the will of God.

We witness the fervor of their faith, their inner strength, their selflessness and their great hope for **"the City which is to come,"** (Eternal life), as stated by St. Paul. (Hebrews 13:14).

In the Byzantine tradition, the Iconographer purposely elongates the bodies and features so that the observer will not be absorbed so much by the human nature, but by the spiritual, as transfigured by Grace. The figures are quite similar. Mouths are small and closed, as a reminder for all to exercise care when we speak.

High foreheads, — large, widely-set eyes reflect the wisdom and beauty of God's Grace. The body is de-emphasized by the voluminous folds of the garments.

We may add here, that El Greco, a Cretan, named Domenicos Theotokopoulos, was strongly influenced by the Byzantine Iconography, as we can see in his masterpieces .

The two dimensional perspective is used by design, in order to transfer one's mind from the worldly to the Divine. Apparent distortions are intentional.

The flat gold background symbolizing the Heavens, allows concentration only on the Image. We can rightfully say, that there is a traditional science when it comes to Byzantine Iconography.

3. The third consideration, is to understand the Icon's role in the life of the Orthodox Christian.

The Church Fathers in the eighth Century stated that the spirit can attain perception of the Divine through the Icons; that is, **we reach the spiritual through the visual.** Therefore, Icons are more than works of religious art. They are a means to grow closer to God, and therefore are considered Holy Objects.

Icons are described as **"Windows to Heaven,"** because they function as a path for dynamic interaction with the Holy Personages venerated.

We pray to the Saints, as having found favor with God to intercede for us, the sinners that we are. Again I repeat here, that the *"window"* (the Icon) offers a place within the secular reality of our hectic daily routines to contemplate the spiritual reality of God's Word, and its role in our lives.

✳
Unexpected, and Believed!

I believe that God, the Source of all power and wisdom, has never stopped bringing *"Miraculous Signs"* and happenings to those who have eyes to see, and ears to hear. He continues, even in our modern Century of technological progress, when everything seems to be measured by the power and force of the material, to bring before us *"Signs"* and *"Miracles"* unexpectedly, in order to awaken us from our spiritual lethargy, and to bring us back to the path from which we have strayed.

The Holy Orthodox Church, with Her unbroken linkage in all respects to the Miraculous Day of the Pentecost, has witnessed the Power of God's guiding Hand through the Centuries.

It is this Power, which was strongly felt in the Spring of 1960, within the Parish boundaries of the St. Paul's Greek Orthodox Cathedral in Hempstead, Long Island.

A simple appearing expression, — like the tears of our *"All-Holy Mother"* emanating from the eyes of a lithographed portrayal was most dynamic and all-powerful, confounding even the wise, who could offer no explanation, other than it could not be proven scientifically.

To be sure, scientific endeavors belong to man's physical and mental counterpart, whereas true faith, which has clear spiritual vision, comprehends the intangible through a person's spiritual counterpart, the soul, and brings one in communication with our Creator.

I stated in the Preface, that as the Pastor of St. Paul's Greek Orthodox Cathedral in Hempstead, N.Y. from 1950-1963, I fully lived the most unusual, unexpected and soul-stirring experiences of the three weeping Icons of the *"All-Holy Mother and Ever-Virgin Mary,"* as they did happen respectively in the homes of two of my Parishioners.

I am a living testimony of all the relative Events, as also are to a sizeable degree, the hundreds of dedicated Parishioners, who volunteered and worked diligently to accommodate the hundreds of thousands who made the pilgrimage to St. Paul's to view the Icons — some to revere and pray, — and others out of sheer curiosity.

However, the chronicles of my experiences are much deeper, because of the fact that daily from morning until nightfall at intervals, I closely studied the Manifestations of the Icons as perhaps no other person did. I humbly make this statement and qualify it with one example.

Hundreds of thousands filed by the three Icons, but did anyone take time to notice the size of the tears, as compared to that of the eyes pictured on the three Icons? I would doubt it very much, simply because all tears were in proportion to the eyes, and nothing looked abnormal.

To my knowledge, only one Reporter, Martin Steadman mentioned in his article, that the tears of the *"Portaitissa"* Icon were in proportion to the eyes. (p. 87). It was indeed a keen observation.

But personally, having lived the experience of the Icons very closely every day, I was continually amazed and truly marveled at the *"Divine Signs."*

It wasn't coincidence by any measure, that the tears of each of the three Icons were in proportion to the size of the eyes of each Icon. This was for me at least, a very powerful testimony and proof of the *"Signs from Above,"* simple as these may have appeared.

It would have been most unnatural to see an Icon with small eyes having disproportionately huge tears emanating from the tear ducts, as it would have been to see tiny tears emerge from large eyes. Most definitely, the tears were in perfect proportion to the size of the eyes of each Icon.

That is the answer, as to why each portrayal and expression appeared very normal to the viewers, and there were never any comments made to the contrary, simply because everything looked so natural, and was in proportion.

Moreover, as you too will learn, the flow of tears on the lithographed Icon prints amazed, and I may say even rendered speechless, the seasoned Reporters of the Metropolitan New York Newspapers, whose work surely exposes them to so many unusual happenings. I really was elated and most gratified by the reverence the Reporters displayed in their interviews, as well as their objective and factual reporting in their articles regarding the Holy Icons.

✳

The 3 Tearing Icons

The first Icon, which shed tears in the apartment of

The *"Mother of Sorrows"*

Mr. & Mrs. Peter Catsounis in Island Park, Long Island was of the Western Christian tradition, showing the lamenting profile of the *"All-Holy Mother"* weeping for the sufferings and crucifixion of Her Son. It is known as *the "Mother of sorrows."*

The artist on his original painting had painted a single tear dripping down the cheek of the Ever-Virgin. Now, from the lithographed print of the Icon, the *"Mother of sorrows"* had shed real tears in the upstairs apartment of Peter and Pagona Catsounis.

The second Icon which shed tears in the apartment of Mr. & Mrs. Peter Koulis in Oceanside is a lithographed copy of the *"All-Holy Mother and Ever-Virgin Mary"* holding the Christ Child.

This Icon is known as the *"Panagia Portaitissa."* (Greek, for '*Mother of the Portals, or Gate.'*) The original Miraculous Icon is enshrined in the *"Katholikon,"* (the main Church of a Monastery) of the Monastery of Iveron,

The *"Panagia Portaitissa"* shed tears April 14, 1960 while Antonia Koulis was praying.

on Mount Athos in Greece. The story of this Holy Icon is fascinating, as it is interesting. It is described later in this Book, after the visit in the Koulis home in Oceanside, L.I. (page 116).

The *"Mother of Perpetual Help"* Icon commenced tearing May 7, 1960 in the home of Peter and Antonia Koulis.

The third Icon, which was given to Mr. & Mrs. Peter Koulis is also a lithographed copy of the original Icon, now enshrined in the Roman Catholic Church of St. Alphonsus in Rome. The Roman Catholics revere this Icon as *"The Mother of Perpetual Help,"* but to the Orthodox it is known as *"The Hodegetria"* (Greek, for one who directs, or shows the way). It is also known as *"The Mother of Mercy."*

"The Hodegetria" Icon is a product of the Cretan School of Iconography. It is a veritable Byzantine Icon, with Greek letters on the painting. Later on in this book you will learn of its history, its theological content and how it got to Rome. (p. 136).

This particular Icon I had given to Peter and Antonia Koulis as a present, to replace the tearing *"Portaitissa"* Icon which they had given to St. Paul's.

The First Manifestation

The Headline spread across the front page of the Sunday edition, March 20, 1960, of the **LONG ISLAND PRESS** stated: *"HUNDREDS FLOCK TO SEE WEEPING MADONNA."* Shock waves were sensed by its subscribing public! Under the headline, there appeared the picture of the lamenting Holy Mother Mary, or *"Mother of Sorrows."* (see page 22). It was the first such *"Happening"* in the history of America.

It created vast repercussions throughout the sophisticated New York City area, and via the Media, the world over. A different type of an Event from those of our every day experiences had come in our midst, and as a result, changes were surely about to ensue in the hearts of many.

The concise statements and testimony of the many eyewitnesses of actual tears flowing from the eyes of the lithographed picture of the Icon of the *"All-Holy Mother"* were included in three lines under the headline as follows:

- **A Reporter saw them.**
- **A Greek Orthodox Priest saw them.**
- **Hundreds of people flocking from all over Long Island jammed into the little three room apartment to see them.**

It all began with a phone call from the owners of the Icon, Peter and Pagona Catsounis asking to speak to me, their Pastor. The call was received during the very hour we were praying the second Friday night Service of the *"Akathist Hymn,"* one of the five similar Services of Lent.

Coincidentally, these Services are dedicated to the *"All-Holy Mother and Ever-Virgin Mary,"* and are held in all Orthodox Churches throughout the world.

These Services are titled, *"The Akathist Hymn."* (*"Akathist"* - Greek, meaning *"not seated."*) Initially this Service was offered as a devotion of gratitude for the *"All-Holy Mother's"* protection during the siege of Constantinople, almost 1400 years ago. This historic Event of so many centuries ago, as you will read below, remains vivid in the minds of the Orthodox through *"The Akathist Hymn"* to this very day.

Since this Service dedicated to the *"All-Holy Mother"* coincided with the tearing Icon 40 years ago, I think it is of sufficient interest to bring to you briefly its history. It constitutes a vital point in the life of Eastern Orthodox Christianity.

�֍

Pertinent Historical Facts
Relatively to the *"Akathist Hymn"*

Initially, I must emphasize that the many devotional Services containing hundreds of hymns offered to the *"Theotokos"* are almost as ancient as the Christian Church! And why not? After all, is She not unique in the history of mankind?

Did She not become the link between Heaven and Earth? Was She not the chosen Vessel of God, through which the Gates of Heaven were opened once again, after they had been closed with the fall of man?

The *"All-Holy Theotokos"* has always held a very special and distinct place in the religious life of every Orthodox Christian. Her Feast Days are important dates on the Christian Orthodox calendar, and are days of obligation.

As the chosen Vessel of God, She is honored and venerated with special devotion. She is described as, more honorable than the Cherubim and more glorious than the Seraphim, both Orders of Angelic Hosts. (Psalm 99:1, Isaiah 6:2)

She stands above all mortals as the first among Saints, and the first in the enjoyment of the glory and blessedness of God. It is with so much love that we address Her as *"Panagia."* We see this extensively in the centuries-old Service held in the Orthodox Churches during the first five Fridays in Lent, titled ***"The Akathist Hymn."*** This unusual title resulted from an historical incident in the Capital of the vast Byzantine Empire, Constantinople.

In the year 626 A.D. the Byzantine Emperor Heracleios had set out on an expedition to stem the aggression of the Persians in the Middle East, and also to retrieve the Holy Cross which the Persians had taken when they had overrun Jerusalem. Fortunately, he was successful.

However in the Emperor's absence, unexpectedly there appeared a threatening enemy outside the great walls of Constantinople. These barbaric hordes were mostly Avars of the tribal Huns. Their siege of Constantinople, which lasted a few months, was very threatening, mainly because of the absence of the troops on their expedition to contain the Persians.

It was gradually becoming apparent that the outnumbered troops, which had remained in the *"Queen City,"* as Constantinople was known, were reaching the point of desperation with thoughts of capitulating. The great wall built around the City could not guarantee security in the long term.

However, the story of David and Goliath once again was destined to come into play. The great faith of the outnumbered troops of the *"Queen City"* would bring about that, which a short time before was considered impossible.

The troops defending the City may have been greatly outnumbered, but their faith was substantially bolstered after seeing the Venerable Patriarch of Constantinople Sergios, along with Clergy, and the high Official of Byzantium, Vonos. Their march along the great walls of Constantinople was continuous, giving the fighting men the needed spirit

The Icon of the *"All-Holy Theotokos"* was held high, and chants of hymns in Her honor were repeatedly heard. The faith of the fighting soldiers was greatly rekindled. They received great courage seeing the Icon, and believed strongly that the prayers for the intercession of the *"Panagia"* would give them renewed strength to stave off the enemy.

It wasn't long after the procession of the Church and Civil Dignitaries along the walls of Constantinople that the miracle came to pass! The chronicler describes the great tempest that suddenly arose in the sea around Constantinople, besieged by the flotilla of the Avars. The unexpected, huge tidal waves literally destroyed the fleet, and the enemy was now in full retreat.

In gratitude, the faithful of Constantinople spontaneously converged to the Church of the *"Theotokos"* at Vlachernae on the Golden Horn. With the Patriarch Sergios officiating, they prayed all night chanting the praises of the Virgin Mary without sitting. Hence the title of the Hymn ***"The Akathist."***

This is part of the great glory of the Holy Orthodox Church. Faith in our Almighty God has always been primary. Veneration also to the *"Holy Mother,"* as well as the Great Heroes of God who found favor with Him, and whom the Church reveres as Saints, for purposes of emulation and intercession.

Without question, the prime Personality in this Galaxy of Saints, is none other than our *"All-Holy Mother St. Mary, the Ever-Virgin."* She is the Mother of all, who seek Her love and protection.

"The Akathist Hymn"

This centuries-old Service is prayed in all the Greek Orthodox Parishes throughout the world.

"The Akathist Hymn," Service has been prayed in the Orthodox Churches since 626 A.D. A note of interest is, that although the separation of the Eastern and Western Churches was already 7 centuries old, Pope Benedict XIV on may May 4, 1746 granted an indulgence of 50 days to the Latin and Eastern Rite Catholics for every recitation of the *"Akathist Hymn."*

This Hymn was rediscovered some decades ago by our sister Roman Catholic Church. In 1934, an eminent Roman Catholic Priest in London, England, Fr. McNabb, discovered *"The Akathist Hymn,"* and translated it into English. However, the book was never republished. Worthy of note is the comment Fr. McNabb expressed when he had discovered this Masterpiece. He stated: *"No apology is needed for introducing 'The Akathist Hymn' to the Christian West. Indeed the West might well be apologetic about of its neglect, or ignorance of such a liturgical and literary masterpiece!"* Very pleased to read this beautiful acceptance, I was surprised why Fr. McNabb had not made any reference to Pope Benedict, who knew about the *'Akathist Hymn'* in the middle of the 18th Century!"

Personally, I too felt the great need for our Church in America to have a translation of *"The Akathist Hymn"* from Greek to English, so that our bi-lingual Congregations would be better served. I was happy to have completed this project in 1970. My translation has been for me, a source of spiritual fulfillment to have accomplished this work.

It is easily understood why Fr. McNabb had such high and due regard for *"The Akathist Hymn."*

One is literally absorbed and truly inspired by this poetic and liturgical masterpiece. It is replete with numerous vivid expressions describing the role of the *"Theotokos"* in God's great plan, by which He would give the opportunity to everyone, to return to the state for which we were created, but fell. Each of the 144 descriptive poetic phrases hailing the *"Theotokos"* in this Hymn, literally constitutes a subject for an artist to paint a mural.

To demonstrate how appropriately and eloquently She is described through illustrative portrayals, I quote here, only two from the 144, to give you some idea of the spiritual wealth of this Hymn:

"Hail To You, — for You are the Throne of the King. Hail! For you bear Him, Who bears the Universe!"

and: **"Hail O Heavenly Ladder, by which God descended. Hail O Bridge, which conveys us from earth to Heaven!"**

Such similar and comparable poetic, descriptive phrases of the *"Theotokos"* continue to successively unfold, becoming like an inexhaustible and refreshing fountainhead, gushing forth pure and refreshing crystal water out of a mountainside.

"The Akathist Hymn" Service links us so vividly to a great and glorious period of Christian History, unknown to most of the Western World. It is a very vibrant tradition, continuously observed in the Orthodox Church since 626 A.D., when the Service of *"The Akathist Hymn"* was prayed for the first time.

The *"Theotokos"* is front and center in this Hymn, because She is the main intercessor to Her Son and our God for our Salvation. — She is the most exalted and most honored Person, who has been so uniquely blessed by God. — She is the most revered and most loved by humans. — She is a binding force for all Christians. — She is the Unique Personality of the world, because of the unique fact of the Lord's Incarnation. — She is the Daughter of Grace; and the Crystal Vessel of Grace by the Holy Spirit. That is why, as children of God, we so readily turn to Her as our loving and protecting Mother.

We return to the First Manifestation

The *"Sign from Above"* was manifested at the *"Family Altar"** of Peter and Pagona Catsounis' home on the evening of March 16, 1960. Pagona, as was her practice every evening knelt in prayer before the Icon on her *"Iconostasis."* She found great comfort, as she told me, expressing her worries, her concerns, her hopes, — and no less the nostalgia for her loved ones in Greece, from whom she had parted only a few months before. But her prayer on this particular evening was indescribably different. It was destined to herald a tiding, which never before had happened in America.

While praying, as she later described her awesome experience, she noticed a tear-drop sourcing from the left eye and rolling down the cheek of the *"All-Holy Mother's"* Icon.

She was understandably shaken by this sudden and unexpected *"happening."* She stood motionless, — fully entranced by what she was seeing. Later she related to me

---

The"Family Altar"* or *"Prayer Corner"* in homes is usually referred to as *"The Iconostasis,"* because it is there, that the Icons are placed.

that she became speechless. Her eyes were wide open — her heart pounding ever loudly! But, she seemed to lack the basic strength to even raise her head to continue viewing the Icon of the *"All-Holy Mother."*

It was a *"happening"* impossible to describe in human terms. One would have to live it to be able to fully comprehend it, after being confronted with such a *Manifestation!*

This inexplicable *Manifestation* seemed to have kept her entranced for a long period of time. She felt totally removed from the physical, and completely absorbed in the spiritual realm. After a while she called her husband Peter.

He too, witnessed the same *Phenomenon* in complete amazement.

"We just remained there on our knees," Pagona told me. "We were silent, and kept looking at the tears of the Icon, and at each other." Even though the hour was rather late, she felt that she had to call her relatives living nearby to come to view the Icon and to be with them.

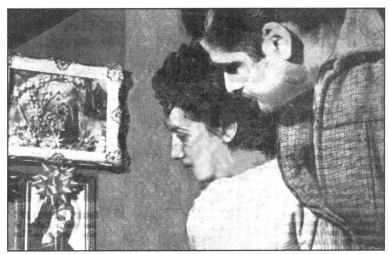

Peter and Pagona Catsounis after their prayers take a closer look at the Icon the *"Mother of Sorrows"* while She continued to shed tears.

She said it was too much for her to handle, having kept her in a very pensive mood.

The next day she had to report to her work. Her co-workers didn't see the Pagona that they were used to seeing. She just wasn't the same. They questioned her, thinking that something might have happened to her, but she still remained rather silent, reasoning that even if she was able to express what she had seen and felt, she would not be understood.

However, Pagona did communicate the *Manifestation* to one of her closest friends. After discussing the matter, she decided that she should call the Pastor at St. Paul's. In the meantime, it wasn't long before the word began circulating, and people commenced to converge at her small apartment in Island Park to view the *Phenomenon*.

Already it was the second Friday evening in Lent, the 18th of March. In retrospect, I am convinced that the tearing of the Icon could not have been a mere coincidence, as having happened during Lent, when we pray those special Services revering our *"Holy Mother."*

Thus, while I was lauding the *"All-Holy Mother's"* virtues from *"The Akathist Hymn,"* (as prayed during the first 5 Fridays in Lent), with over 500 worshippers at the Service, Pagona Catsounis had phoned to state that the Icon of the *"Panagia"* was tearing.

She wanted to speak to me personally. The Secretary reassured her that I would return her call soon after the Service.

Truthfully, it had been a very long day, tending to various duties and culminating with the Service of *"The Akathist Hymn."* As I was preparing to leave for home, the Secretary informed me that Mrs. Catsounis had frantically called to tell me that the Icon of the *"All-Holy Mother"* was tearing. Hearing this strange news, I did not know how to accept it, or what to believe.

My thoughts wandered. They wandered, because in the three decades of serving our Church in the Metropolitan New York area I had heard of parallel, unusual situations. All of these usually turned out to be subjective, rather than objective. However, I want to state that by no means am I a doubting Thomas; but regarding this situation I don't think anyone will disagree, that one would have to see to believe, because of the unimaginable and unusual nature of an Icon weeping, — a Manifestation, that until March 16, 1960 was unheard of in this Country!

As was my practice to never refuse any call to respond and to serve, I called Mrs. Catsounis. Sounding somewhat uncontrolled in her emotions, I reassured her that I would drive down to view the *Phenomenon!*

It was about 10:00 p.m. when I arrived at Peter and Pagona Catsounis' apartment. Seeing the long line of parked cars and the hundreds of people gathered outside of the house, I was amazed at how quickly the news had already circulated.

It was a chore to get to the house. The many parked cars and the people shoulder to shoulder had filled the street, waiting for their turn to walk up the stairs into the small apartment to view the Icon. Outside of the house were two Police cars with the flashing red lights rotating.

The Police were busy directing the people to orderly enter the apartment of Peter and Pagona Catsounis.

As soon as I entered the front door I sensed the fragrance of the incense used in the Orthodox Churches and homes. Ascending the flight of stairs I was welcomed by Peter and Pagona. Their faces reflected the strain of the endless hours in greeting and speaking with the hundreds of people parading through their apartment to view the Icon. They led me to their *"Family Altar,"* to show me the Icon.

Without any idea of what I was about to encounter, I found myself standing before the Icon in complete awe!

How could I ever have envisioned that, which I now was really seeing! Standing motionless before the Icon for a few moments, I saw a tear forming from one of the eyes, and gradually dropping to roll down the cheek of the *"All-Holy Mother"* onto Her garment, and down to the bottom edge of the lithographed Icon.

This Icon of the *"All-Holy Mother"* had deep sentimental value for the Catsounis couple. They treasured it because it was a wedding gift from their aunt, a Nun in a Greek Orthodox Monastery in their native Chios, Greece. For them it had added significance, especially since they had recently been married, and presently away from their beloved Aunt in Greece, over five thousand miles away. It was for them a precious and lasting bond with their Aunt.

I might insert at this point, that almost in every Orthodox home, there is a *"Prayer Corner"* formally called *"The Iconostasis,"* (where Icons are placed). Besides the Icons, there is a vigil light, before which the daily prayers are said. I would further venture to state that one will probably never find an Orthodox home without an Icon of a Patron Saint, and surely more than often, an Icon of the Holy Mother holding the Christ Child in Her arms.

On the *"Iconostasis,"* (*"Family Altar"*) besides the Icons, there is usually a small hand censer used on various occasions. At times, and especially on Holidays the faithful cense all the rooms of their home reciting prayers.

A small piece of charcoal is ignited to which a few small pieces of aromatic incense are added, giving the fragrance of a religious feeling in the house.

The censer was continuously lighted, emitting aromatic smoke in the Catsounis apartment, and filling it with the fragrance I had sensed, as soon as I had entered through the front door.

The censing for the Orthodox faithful is connected with the Church experience. In all the Orthodox Churches, during the various Rituals and Liturgies, the use of incense is ever present. During specific times in every Service, and especially in the Divine Liturgy, the Priest repeatedly censes all around the Church and the Congregation. This, as well as all practices in the Orthodox Church is Biblically based, as we read in Psalm 141, verse 2:

"Let my prayer be set forth before You as incense; and the lifting up of my hands as the evening sacrifice."

It is symbolic for the Orthodox to use incense in prayer, because as the smoke rises, so also do our prayers rise up to approach the Throne of God.

Having then seen actual tears sourcing from the tear duct, I was overtaken by an indescribable emotion. I had never come close, nor could I ever have envisioned a similar situation. Furthermore, I was deeply moved seeing the expression on the faces of the Catsounis couple, as well as that of their relatives, close friends and neighbors, who had filled that small apartment.

They all reflected an unusual aura of serenity, peace and humility. It was indeed a soul-stirring and heartwarming experience for me; one, which has been indelibly inscribed in my heart and mind.

Among the relatives and very close friends who had gathered to view the Icon, was the Pastor of the famed St. Anthony's Roman Catholic Shrine in nearby Oceanside. For years, thousands of Roman Catholic worshippers had made the pilgrimage to St. Anthony's from all parts of the Country.

Pagona Catsounis introduced me to the Priest as her Pastor. Later, she told me that the Priest had spent a few hours among the people in the apartment conversing with them, and occasionally going to stand silently before the Icon.

After he had left, she related to me that the Priest had approached her with an offer to purchase the Icon for his Shrine.

The Catsounis couple responded that such *Manifestations* do not have a price tag. Still further, that an Icon with this type of *Manifestation* no longer belongs to individuals, but to the Church, for all Christians to revere and be blessed by the *"Panagia."*

Having then witnessed what I considered to be a *"Divine Sign,"* I prayed the *"Paraklesis"* Service, a special Ritual of beseeching the *"Panagia"* to intercede for us to Her Son, our God, to bless and protect us. It was almost midnight on Friday when I departed.

Early Saturday morning I called the Archdiocese to speak to the spiritual Head of our Church, Archbishop Iakovos, only to be informed that he had traveled to Springfield, Massachusetts to celebrate the Liturgy at St. George's Greek Orthodox Church.

I then called the Priest in Springfield at intervals for information as to where I could possibly contact the Archbishop, but there was no answer. In those days there were no phone answering devices to leave a message.

After many attempts I finally established contact with His Eminence in the late afternoon, and commenced relating to him the happenings. He was totally astounded to hear of this *Phenomenon,* and listened intently.

His Eminence had known me since the first day he had arrived from Constantinople as a young Deacon in 1939 to become one of the Professors of our newly founded Theological Seminary in Pomfret Center, Connecticut, in which I was already in my third year of study. Knowing me well for over 20 years, he knew that I was not only a believer, but also a pragmatist.

Respectfully, I suggested that he interrupt his visit in Springfield and come to Long Island to be present as the head of our Church, at this first *"Manifestation"* in America. I emphasized that it was a *"Sign,"* which had all the elements of the *Mysterious* and *Miraculous,* having come from *Above.*

I must confess, that I was very disappointed when His Eminence informed me, that he would not alter his schedule.

Before ending our conversation he told me to meet him at the Kennedy Airport on Monday evening to drive him to Island Park, which I did. This was now Monday evening, March 21, 1960.

As we were approaching the Catsounis residence it didn't surprise me to see the street overflowing with even more people than on the two previous evenings. The Archbishop though, had never expected to witness what he saw. He was really astonished seeing the multitudes.

With the help of the Police we were able make our way to reach the house. I did notice that His Eminence was visibly taken aback witnessing the scene, never having imagined such an overwhelming response.

Entering the apartment His Eminence was welcomed by Peter and Pagona Catsounis, who escorted him to the *"Family Altar"* where the Weeping Icon was located. By this time the tearing had stopped.

It was significant however, and clearly visible, that a small bead from the last tear, which began to source but did not drop, had become crystallized, sparkling like a tiny diamond in the corner of the eye. I pointed this out to his Eminence, and that from that particular corner of the eye the tears had been emanating.

He stood silently in contemplation, staring at the Icon for some time. The apartment was filled to capacity with relatives and friends of the Catsounis couple, yet there was a deadening silence. His Eminence began the *"Paraklesis"* Service, after which he spoke briefly on the role of *"Panagia"* in God's master plan of having chosen Her to become the Vessel, through which the Saviour of mankind would receive His human form, to ultimately become the *"ransom for many"* to save us.

In closing, he announced that I was to visit the Catsounis home every Wednesday for one year to pray the *"Paraklesis"* Service.

His Eminence Archbishop Iakovos takes a closer look at the Icon of the *"Mother of Sorrows,"* as Fr. George Papadeas and Pagona Catsounis look on.

Also, that I was to bring the Icon to St. Paul's in Hempstead on Wednesday, March 23rd to be enshrined.

When the Icon was in the tearing stage for three days, no one could have ever known how long it would continue to shed tears. I am really sorry that His Eminence did not make the trip in time to have seen for himself, what so many hundreds had seen in the three previous days in the Catsounis home.

The spiritual effect on the people of all Faiths was gratifying to witness. Some of these feelings were published in the Newspapers. For instance, in the **WORLD TELEGRAM and SUN** on March 21, 1960, there was an article submitted by their Reporter describing the *"Manifestation."*

He mentioned, that while the people waited outside the Catsounis apartment, it was notable that there was a woman who said she had an illness and thought perhaps the Holy Mother pictured on the Icon would help her.

She refused to give her name, but said she was of the Jewish faith.

In the same article, another woman from the neighborhood said: "You come in skeptical, but you see it happen, and there is a sensation that is hard to explain."

"People who see it, leave with a feeling they've seen something they'll never forget, but they'll never be able to explain it."

In the **NEW YORK JOURNAL AMERICAN,** Thursday March 24, 1960, among other items regarding the Catsounis' Icon it was reported that: "A trinity of white sea gulls, soaring against the blue sky over Island Park, L.I. have heralded the enshrinement of the *'Madonna of the Tears'."*

"Some observers said it was no mere coincidence that the three gulls appeared overhead, just as the Weeping Icon of the Madonna was taken in procession to St. Paul's Greek Orthodox Cathedral in Hempstead."

"The Rev. George L. Papadeas, Pastor of St. Paul's, reverently took the Icon from the small bedroom shrine in the apartment of Mr. & Mrs. Peter Catsounis at 41 Norfolk Rd., Island Park, N. Y."

"The gulls were spotted flying over the house, and a woman in the crowd said excitedly, 'Look at the birds. It's a good omen'!"

"The birds of good portent 'escorted' the procession of 30 cars to Hempstead and circled over the Church while the Service was being conducted inside."

In a similar vein, the story of the first Weeping Icon was reported in all the major Metropolitan New York Newspapers. To print the contents of these articles would be somewhat repetitious. However, I was additionally surprised to have received from a friend living in Athens, Greece a two column article, reporting the facts, as we had read them in our Newspapers here.

The caption read: **GREEK AMERICAN NEWS: "The Crying Madonna,"** reported by George J. Karamanos.

The news had spread all over the world via the syndicated networks. I received so many clippings from cities around the Country reporting the events of the Weeping Icon, which in fact we were personally experiencing.

Imagine my surprise one day, when I received a ceramic dinner plate from Tokyo, Japan with the Icon of the Madonna etched in the center. This proved one thing — that the hearts of people, — regardless of race, color, or creed have a spiritual thirst, and are receptive to spiritual expressions and manifestations.

Unfortunately, it is we humans who put up roadblocks — that is, — we permit the things and cares of this world to detour or divert the spiritual. As a result, we allow the spiritual to knuckle under the weight of the our material possessions, worldly pursuits, discoveries for scientific progress, and the like. A natural question arises: "Could it be, that this is the reason many feel so empty, regardless of the many comforts and possessions they have in life?"

I have no doubt that *"Signs from Above,"* which defy the laws or nature, and therefore are supernatural, cannot in any way be explained in human terms. They are most certainly a reality and have a specific purpose, which we must come to believe.

These *"Signs"* constitute seeds, which are meant to be planted and to flourish in human hearts. They can only germinate and bear a wealth of spiritual fruits, if they fall into fertile *"soil"* of human hearts. It is then that miracles commence to happen in life.

Of this, we are reminded of the seeds in the Parable of the Sower, (Matthew 13:3-9), which is befitting to mention at this point. In this Parable of the Lord we make note of the various types of *"soil,"* witnessed in human hearts, so true to life.

I chose to make reference here of this Parable, because the *Manifestation* of the Holy Icons was a seed planted in people's hearts. But, — did this seed actually germinate? Let us understand the picture from the Parable of our Lord.

The Parable commences with this phrase: **"A sower went out into the field to sow his seeds."** As we know, a seed to germinate requires not only fertile soil, but also cultivation and care to grow, so that it may give forth its fruit. In the Parable, **"some seeds fell by the wayside and the fowls came and devoured them up."** These seeds having fallen by the wayside could never have produced, because the soil had become firm from the trampling on the roadway.

The compacted soil represents those, who have distanced themselves from the warmth of God's love.

Through their repetitive acts, contrary to moral principles, they have permitted their hearts to become somewhat hardened, so that we could say that they hardly have a conscience.

"Some seeds fell in a rocky area. The seeds began to sprout, but soon they wilted and dried up because of the lack of moisture."

This rocky area represents those, who hear and receive the word of God, and initially appear to be enthusiastic.

However, only too soon this enthusiasm wanes, simply because they neglect or minimize their spiritual counterpart.

They refuse to consciously dig up and cast away from their heart the stones of egotism, arrogance, avarice, greed, slander, hypocrisy, selfishness and other plagues of mankind, so that the soil of their heart can become more fertile. Consequently, the soil of their heart soon becomes dry, preventing the seed of God's love to germinate and to give forth its desired fruit.

"The third group of seeds fell in better soil, but here there were many small weeds and thorns. The seeds blossomed and the plants seemed very promising, but the weeds and thorns soon outgrew and choked them, so that they wilted and dried up."

In this group, are those Christians who seek to serve two masters simultaneously. They want to be loyal and serve God, but at the same time they permit the worldly pursuits to prevail, which may be the insatiable desire to amass material things, — or the struggle to be recognized above others, — or the self gratification that intellectually they are superior to others, — or the perpetual competition to outdo all others, and the like. These *"weeds"* virtually overgrow and choke the plants of true happiness and fulfillment, because they will not permit the word of God to fully bloom in their hearts and bring forth a bountiful harvest of spiritual fruits.

"The fourth group of seeds fell in rich and fertile soil." That is in Christian hearts, which not only hear the word of God, but conscientiously translate the Lord's teachings into deeds.

They not only receive the seeds in the fertile soil of their hearts, but take extra care to cultivate them. As a result, these seeds, as the Bible concludes in the Parable, **"give forth fruits one hundred fold."**

What this world then desperately needs is fertile Christian soil, as in the fourth category; — for the seeds of the Lord's love to be planted, to germinate, to be cultivated and nourished, so as to give forth fruits, which would result in personal fulfillment, and in turn to be of general benefit to mankind.

The First Holy Icon is brought to St. Paul's

As had been requested by Archbishop Iakovos, I had set the wheels into motion to bring the Holy Icon to St. Paul's on Wednesday, March 23, 1960 with all the reverence and dignity possible. I was thankful that a friend had offered me the use of his limousine, realizing that with my vestments and holding the Holy Icon adorned with a wreath of flowers might have been somewhat cumbersome in a regular sedan.

Fully vested, I proceeded early Wednesday morning followed by Parishioners in their cars, who wanted to take part in this procession from the Catsounis apartment. There were about 20 cars following the limousine to the Catsounis home.

On that very morning, as is the case with all the Wednesdays and Fridays during the Lenten period, the Divine Liturgy of the Pre-Sanctified Gifts had been scheduled. This holds true for all the Orthodox Churches throughout the world.

On the preceding Sunday, March 20th, 1960 after the Divine Liturgies at St. Paul's, I had announced to both Congregations that the tearing Icon would be brought to St. Paul's on Wednesday, March 23rd, 9:00 a.m. to be blessed and enshrined, through the solemn Divine Liturgy of the Pre-Sanctified Gifts. I had asked everyone to make every possible effort to come and receive the blessing of the *Divine Sign.*

It was a beautiful day; one of the first in the new Spring season. Arriving at the Catsounis home in Island Park a little after 8:00 a.m., we saw quite a few people of the St. Paul's Membership there, wanting to join the motorcade to the Church.

Making the sign of the cross, I reverently took the flower adorned Icon from the Catsounis home to the limousine for the half hour trip to the Church with more than 30 cars in the entourage

When we arrived in front of the

Fr. George Papadeas steps from from the Catsounis home with the *"Holy Icon"* for the trip to the St. Paul's Cathedral. Peter Catsounis follows.

Church I was deeply touched and immensely pleased to have seen the hundreds of our Parishioners on the patio awaiting our arrival.

As soon as the limousine stopped, before the door was opened for me to step out with the *"Holy Icon,"* momentarily I glanced out the window at the hundreds standing on the elevated patio in front of the Church. It was then, — during a split-second moment, — that I was astonished to have seen three white birds, which looked like doves in a triangular formation, swiftly swooping down over the people almost touching their heads.

The Parishioners in automatic reflex response, seeing the birds swooping down toward them bowed their heads. I heard them almost like a choir in unison exclaim loudly with a gasp, at this most unusual and unexpected happening.

The appearance of the three white doves in formation was for me a visible, caressed blessing from *"Above."*

Before I was able to step from the limousine, John Paul the President of the Parish Council who was following the lead car, bursting with excitement rushed up to me and said: *"did you see the birds?"*

I responded, *"of course I did. I saw them swoop over the heads of our Parishioners, gathered to receive us."* He said: *"No! No! I didn't mean that. I'm talking about the three white birds, which looked like doves flying in a triangular formation over the limousine. From the very moment we departed from Island Park, they came out of nowhere, and were flying over the limousine like escorts all the way to the Church."*

In all his excitement he didn't stop to think of how could I ever have been able to see anything, if it was over the top of the limousine!

However, hearing John Paul's witness, and after seeing the people bowing their heads because of the three birds swooping down toward them, it was obvious that this was another *"Sign from Above"* blessing our people.

For me, it was symbolic of the Holy Trinity granting us an unique and exceptionally Divine Blessing!

After flying down over the people's heads I saw the doves flying away. Little did any of us know while in Church, that the doves would have returned to continue blessing us from above the Church for about three hours, as was testified.

The Holy Orthodox Church by no means is lacking in tradition. In fact, it is so prolific in this sphere. It respects so many and varied symbolisms, whose chief purpose is to bring us in closer communication with God.

For instance, there were three white doves. Why three, and flying in a triangular formation? Why not two, or one? Also, as scheduled according to our Rubrics, on Wednesdays and Fridays in Lent we celebrate one of our seven Sacraments, the Liturgy of the Pre-sanctified Gifts. Indeed the Supreme Sacrament, bringing us closer in communion with God.

Again, for myself who is prone to classify symbolism above coincidence, another number became prominent in my mind, which I considered more than coincidence. Besides the three Priests serving the St. Paul Parish we had four visiting Priests for a total of seven, who came to participate in the Divine Liturgy that Wednesday morning.

Seven Priests! Another sacred number I thought to myself, bringing to my mind our seven Sacraments!

Symbolisms? Coincidences? — Regardless, — all the pieces fit perfectly together, to form a most precious spiritual picture. Shortly before any indication of the *"Sign"* of the tearing Icon came to us, Fr. George Kambanis, having recently arrived from the Island of Rhodes, was assigned to

St. Paul's as an Assistant Priest. God had gifted him with a resonant baritone voice. It was always such a pleasure to hear him chant our hymns.

Proceeding to enter St. Paul's for the enshrining of the Holy Icon of the *"Mother of Sorrows."* Fr. George Kambanis far right, Elias Papadeas holding the Processional Cross.
Fr. Dean Theodore of Blue Point holding the Holy Bible followed by Fr. George Papadeas carrying the Holy Icon.

I often had said, that if Fr. Kambanis wasn't a Priest, he surely could have qualified for the Opera.

Everyone now was ready to join in the procession to enter the Church. The Choir was followed by the Altar Boys holding the Processional Cross, the Fans of the Seraphim (six-winged Angels), and the candlesticks. The Clergy and the Congregation followed. We proceeded in groups down the center aisle. The Congregation gradually filled the pews.

Entering the Church, the Clergy with the Laity commenced singing the *"Kontakion"* (Canticle) of *"The Akathist Hymn"* Service. This hymn expresses the gratitude of the Christians of Constantinople to the Holy Theotokos for their miraculous deliverance from the besieging Avars in 626 A.D.

The 1374 year old hymn is as follows:

"Unto You, O Theotokos, the invincible Champion, Your City in thanksgiving ascribes the victory for the deliverance from sufferings. Having Your might unassailable, free me from all dangers, that I may cry unto You: *Hail! O Bride Ever-Virgin!*"

In this hymn, as well as in all those from the inexhaustible wealth of our profound Orthodox hymnology we can readily see, that the Biblical events are closely related to intercessory prayers.

In the the "Catholic" (Greek for *"Universal"*) Epistle of St. James Chapter 5 v 1, we read:

"The effectual fervent prayer of a righteous person availeth much!"

According to this verse, could there ever be a more righteous person than the *"All-Holy Theotokos,"* the loving Mother of all, whose prayers and intercessions are asked by all of us, Her faithful children? In the above hymn the inspired composer of this poetic masterpiece pleads that the *"Theotokos"* will deliver us from all dangers.

Before continuing with the procession in St. Paul's Church for the Liturgy, I think it is pertinent to interject here some relative historical notes.

Some Background Historical Notes

I have always been very nostalgic for the glories of Orthodoxy in the great historic periods down through the Ages!

So it was, that proceeding down the center aisle of our beautiful and impressive St. Paul's Cathedral holding the Icon of the *"Panagia,"* I felt mentally and spiritually transposed, envisioning the glorious days in the great Cathedral in Constantinople, dedicated to the Divine Wisdom, and known as *"Agia Sophia."*

This huge Cathedral, without question is one of the architectural Wonders of the world, considering that it was constructed about 15 centuries ago, and is still standing intact.

It was the great Emperor of the Byzantine Empire Justinian who conceived the construction of this massive Cathedral, requiring five years to build, 532 to 537 A.D. St. Sophia was the largest Church of united Christendom, until the construction of St. Peter's in Rome, some 1000 years later.

It is estimated that St. Sophia has a capacity of about 15,000 worshippers, whereas St. Peters can accommodate about 25,000.

The Cathedral of *"The Divine Wisdom"* in Constantinople. The minarets were added after 1453 when the Turkish conquerers converted the Cathedral into a Mosque.

This great Monument to the Glory of God, standing intact for almost 1500 years, was the Cathedral, not only for the Eastern Christians, but for the totality of Christendom, because there was no division in the Christian Church then as there is today.

Furthermore, Constantinople was the capital of the vast Byzantine Empire. Here also, from the days of St. Andrew the first called Apostle, is the See of the Ecumenical Orthodox Christian Patriarch in an unbroken lineage, as his successor.

During the Divine Liturgies in this monumental Cathedral, the Emperor's throne from which he followed the Divine Liturgy was located in the north transept, opposite that of the Patriarch's, in the south transept.

Unfortunately, when the Ottoman Turks overran and subjugated the vast Byzantine Empire on May 29, 1453 A.D., this Gem of Orthodoxy became a Moslem Mosque. In recent decades the Turkish Government converted it to a Museum of the Turkish State, whose assigned representatives collect entrance fees from those, who visit this unique Cathedral of Christendom, unparalleled in architecture and Byzantine mosaic Icons.

It is recorded that the Divine Liturgies celebrated in the St. Sophia Cathedral were like bringing Heaven to earth. Describing the Liturgy, the historian registered a 300 voice Choir with the Patriarch officiating, assisted by a host of Bishops, Priests and Deacons; the Emperor always following the Liturgy from his throne.

To have been part of the Congregation in St. Sophia, must have been like having a seat in Heaven.

The inspiring Divine Liturgies could easily enable the spirit of the faithful worshippers to soar to the heights of Heaven.

History has recorded that the Russian Emperor Vladimir wanting to establish a uniform Religion for his new Empire, had sent Emissaries to Churches to various parts of Europe, who would then report to him.

The Emperor would make his decision after hearing the report from his Emissaries. They visited many Churches, and finally attended the Liturgy in the Cathedral of *"The Divine Wisdom "* in Constantinople. They were so moved and inspired, that when they returned to give the Emperor their report they stated: *"When we attended the Liturgy in St. Sophia, we didn't know whether we were still on earth, or had been transported to Heaven."*

The rest is history. Mass conversions and baptisms in 988 A.D. established Orthodox Christianity for all time in the vast Russian Empire.

❊

Back to the Procession
in St. Paul's

So it was, that proceeding down the center aisle of our St. Paul's Cathedral, as I have mentioned — for a very brief moment, I felt myself mentally and spiritually in the midst of the glorious beauty of Constantinople's St. Sophia Cathedral, sensing deeply the grandeur, as well as the mysticism of those centuries long past.

To be sure, I was not in the St. Sophia Cathedral of the Byzantine Capital, but in our very own miniature *"St. Sophia,"* — our beautiful St. Paul's Cathedral, — a microcosmic reflection of the massive and unique Cathedral in Constantinople.

Slowly and reverently walking down the aisle of St. Paul's, the Clergy, the Choir and the Congregation sang in unison the 1400 y e a r o l d h y m n of the *"Theotokos"* (**"Unto You O Theotokos ...."**) with so much fervor, that it produced re-sounding, sonorous and indeed celestial reverberations, bouncing back from the vaulted ceilings and dome of the imposing St. Paul's Byzantine-style Edifice. Fr. Kambanis' resonant baritone voice w a s clearly distinguishable. This Service

Fr. Papadeas proceeding down the center aisle with the Holy Icon *"Mother of Sorrows"* preceded by the Altar Boy Dean Papadeas holding a candlestick. Shown partly in center is James Tricoukes.

was one of the most uplifting, glorious and indescribable spiritual exaltations I have ever experienced.

Forty years may have passed on into history from that most memorable day of March 16, 1960, but in writing this Book I am presently reliving most vividly the Great Events, and more importantly, recording them in this Book for posterity, and for all to learn of them as they truly happened.

The Divine Liturgy of the Pre-Sanctified Gifts on March 23, 1960 was well attended. St. Paul's was filled to capacity. After the Liturgy I spoke briefly regarding the *Manifestation* and among other things I said:

"A Great Sign, and a special Blessing from Above has come to us, — to our Blessed Parish of St. Paul's — and indeed to the World!"

I firmly believed this, as I still do, and sought to transmit it to everyone who had filled our Church on that morning. Following the Liturgy we prayed the *"Paraklesis"* Service. We offered prayers for those present, — for those absent, — and for peace to come to our troubled world. At the end, the Faithful filed by to venerate the Holy Icon, each expressing inwardly what he/she had in their heart. After the last Parishioner had left, it was always my routine to make my inspection all around the Church, and especially the Narthex, lest a candle was left burning etc.

Entering the Narthex, I was approached by three men standing there in their work clothes. They told me that they were Roman Catholics of Italian descent, and were hesitant of walking into Church because of their work clothes. They had been informed of the Weeping Icon from the departing Parishioners, and wanted to see the Icon and to offer their prayers. In speaking with the one whose English was a little better than that of the other two, he related to me that while they were cutting down the diseased tree outside the Church, they couldn't help but notice three white birds in a triangular formation circling the dome continually.

This aroused their curiosity. They knew nothing of what was transpiring inside the

After the *"Paraklesis"* Service, Pagona Catsounis kisses the Holy Bible held by Fr. George Papadeas, while husband Peter waits to be next. Their Holy Icon is framed with flowers. Holding the Processional Cross is Elias Papadeas.

Church, nor the reason for all the activity they were witnessing on a weekday morning.

They kept chopping away at the tree, stopping at times to watch the birds flying around the dome. Their curiosity was ever increasing. They would watch, and then resume their work. The white birds were still in the same formation, endlessly circling the dome. They just could not understand what they were witnessing, because it wasn't natural for birds to be flying in formation for such a long time in a small area. They just could not understand.

While the Parishioners were exiting from the Church, they paused from their work temporarily, and kept looking up at the birds.

After I had related to them the event of the *"Divine Sign"* at the Catsounis home, the worker said: *"You know Father, it had to be from God, because all during the three hours of the Service, the birds kept circling the dome, and flew away after the last Parishioners had left the Church."*

I then told them that these same birds had flown over the limousine from the Catsounis home in Island Park to the Cathedral, and that when we arrived at the Church the birds swooped over the heads of the Parishioners standing on the patio, and flew away.

But, little did I know, that when we entered

Fr. George Papadeas meditating before the Holy Icon, after everyone had left the Service.

the Church for the Liturgy, the three birds had revisited St. Paul's to continue to bless us. What an indescribable Gift!

I was so thrilled to have heard this unsolicited testimony from those three workers. Had they not spoken to me, this additional and very powerful testimony of the three doves flying for three hours around the dome would never have been known.

In retrospect, I am sorry that I didn't have the opportunity to get their comments on tape, or at least ask for, and register their names. At that time, I never thought that a few decades later I would be registering these historical Events.

Nonetheless, this was veritable testimony, as was that of the occupants of the vehicles, who saw the three white doves flying over the limousine all the way on the half hour trip from Island Park to the Church.

Yes, — for me and for countless others, this was much more than a coincidence.

St.Paul's was now a Church crowned with a *"Special Blessing."* A steady and continuous stream of visitors, day after day, kept arriving from near and afar — some to venerate, and others to satisfy their curiosity.

I considered it such a special *"Blessing from Above"* for our St. Paul's Parish to have received the *"Sign"* of the tearing Icon, — the *Blessing* of the three doves, — the opening and closing of the Holy Mother's eyelids and the moving of Her eyes from one side to the other. (see p. 59). It was as though She wanted to see all present, and through them, all Her dedicated and loving children!

I honestly felt that this *"Divine Sign,"* in all its aspects, was a seal of approval for our comparatively young Congregation, which had worked so diligently over the past 10 years since its founding, with unselfish dedication in the true spirit of God's love. It is this love which resulted in bringing to fruition our great Parish dream and so soon!

The construction of a Byzantine-style Church with its adjacent buildings, which present Orthodoxy, the Mother Christian Church with its 2000 year unbroken history, to our fellow Americans in the new World.

From the initial year when we occupied the imposing St. Paul's Parish Complex on the beautiful Cathedral Avenue in Hempstead, it had become a landmark in Nassau County, because of its imposing and indeed outstanding architecture.

It is an Edifice which brought the old world to the new, and which blended so harmoniously with the environment.

The setback of the structures, — the sprawling connected Buildings, — the circular walks, — the beautiful landscape and the multi-color trees enhanced the complex tremendously, thanks to our eminent Architect Mr. Ray Julian, of Syosset.

Although the construction was completed in 1958, I maintained contact with Mr. Julian, who was not only an distinguished architect, but a true friend; and more importantly a devout believer in God. Mr. Julian had dedicated his professional life to strictly designing Churches.

Prior to the construction of St. Paul's, he had taken me to various Churches he had designed. It was easily discernible to see certain characteristics, which distinguished his work. It is this quality had become the deciding factor in our choosing him to design St. Paul's. From our initial meeting he had impressed me as a devout Christian; an inspired individual, who I feel must have done much praying so that his work would result to the best possible for the Glory of God.

He brought to my mind the Monks and Byzantine Iconographers of centuries ago, who would not commence painting an Icon before they had fasted and prayed. It is no wonder that their work, while closely imitated, has never been equaled.

After completing his magnificent work at St. Paul's, bequeathing a true Gem to our Orthodox Church in America, Mr. Julian moved to Charlottesville, Virginia to live on one of those beautiful farms that spot the general area.

Periodically we exchanged letters. On April 20, 1960 among other things he wrote:

"Father, we have been reading about the miracle that has occurred at St. Paul's. My sister even sent me a newspaper clipping from Kentucky, and our friends from Long Island have sent us numerous clippings.

I believe, that this is all Heaven-sent. Even the small beginning we made some years ago, fits into the scheme. If you ever think of building a Shrine, or anything like that, I would like to offer to make the plans and specifications for you without cost. I am sure that Our Lady would reward me in some other way for this work.

My regards to the family, and to all at St. Paul's, and may God bless you in this new found miracle."

Sincerely,

Ray

✳

Officials in Washington to hear First hand of the tearing Icon

The popular and esteemed Senator from New York Mr. Kenneth Keating had extended to me an invitation to offer the opening prayer of a session in the U.S. Senate Chamber, about a month before the unexpected Events of the Icon. The date was set for Thursday, March 24th, 1960.

How could I ever have imagined then, when I had received the invitation, that we would have been blessed with the *"Divine Sign,"* and that it would be the day after we would have brought the Icon to be enshrined in St. Paul's?

As difficult as it appeared for me to be away from St. Paul's, especially on the initial days of the *"Manifestation,"* I was comforted by the fact that I had two Associates, who were able to handle the Church matters efficiently.

Considering the trip to Washington as an opportunity for my two sons, Elias, age 15 and Dean, 12, to see the inner Chambers of our Nation's Capitol, and other historic Buildings in Washington, my wife Bess and I decided to take them with us. The timing was very close. I had made reservations at the Mayflower Hotel with arrival time, about 10:00

p.m. on Wednesday, March 23rd, — the same evening of the many soul-stirring and unforgettable spiritual experiences of that day.

As always it had been a very busy day in Church, holding brief Services and speaking with so many who always approached me to learn more about the Icon.

As much as it pleased me speaking to people of various Faiths, it became necessary for me to set a cut-off time. I had phoned my wife telling her to be packed and prepared to depart promptly at 5:00 p.m.

I would simply honk the horn, pick up my family, and we would be on our way.

As soon as I had pulled into the driveway I was informed by my wife that the Church Secretary had just called, frantically asking that I should not depart for Washington unless I would firstly stop by the Church.

She told my wife that about 20 women, who were keeping a vigil in the Church, had gathered around the little Shrine of the Icon, and were almost hysterical after having seen the eyelids of the Icon of the Virgin opening and closing, and Her eyes moving from side to side.

I was astounded to have heard this new development. It seemed that one mysterious expression was following another. Although our departure time was set, this new "happening" necessitated the witnessing for myself.

There is no question, that if one focuses and stares with complete concentration on a particular object for any length of time, he/she may commence seeing or imagining things, which in reality are not.

To be sure, the mind can become very productive and imaginative, according to circumstances. But, — when more than one person witnesses the same thing at the same time and at first glance on some object, it surely cannot be a figment of the imagination, nor a hallucination.

With my wife and two sons I entered the Church and quickly proceeded down the center aisle.

When the women, the first witnesses of this new *"miraculous"* expression, saw us approaching, they moved aside so that we could approach to see the *"happening"* on the Icon. I was closely followed by my wife Bess, and our two sons.

Words cannot adequately describe the inward jolt, or shock that I felt, upon seeing the eyelids of our *"All-Holy Mother"* slowly opening and closing, and Her eyes moving from side to side continually. It gave us an eerie feeling.

Her eyes were as live and natural as those of us humans. In utter amazement, I looked at my wife, and she at me.

We both saw the identical movement of the eyes and the opening and closing of Her eyelids.

My children, Elias and Dean, moved closer and viewed the identical expression with looks of complete astonishment. Most assuredly, not in the least could it have been a case of imagining or hallucinating.

The four of us at first glance, and at the same time, saw the identical happening, as did those women.

We stood there speechless, — often making the sign of the cross for about ten minutes. We were witnessing an unbelievable *"happening,"* which was steadily continuing.

I was informed later, that this latest *"Miraculous"* expression had continued steadily until after 10:00 p.m. that night. The twenty women had decided to keep an all night vigil in the Church. Our observation had been identical to theirs. Understandably, they were overcome by emotion, and with tears flowing from their eyes, they had frantically vented their emotions while blessing themselves repeatedly.

Relatively reporting, *"in 1796,"* according to the Roman Catholic Magazine *'Divine Love,'* *"there had been more than one instance, where many eye-witnesses saw the eyes of the Virgin Mary move from side to side on Icons of the 'All-Holy Mother' in Churches around Rome."*

It was, as stated at that time, *"a forewarning of things to happen very soon. Pope Pius VI having been informed of the eyes moving on many Madonna Icons, appointed a special Commission to investigate."*

"The appointees of Pope Pius VI contacted the 26 Churches, and verified the action reported on the Icons of the Madonna. The Pope then proclaimed the events "miraculous," and signed a declaration to that effect on February 28, 1797 A.D."

"In 1796, Napoleon with his French army invaded the Papal States. Exactly one year after the Pope had proclaimed the Events of the Madonna's eyes moving side to side, that is on February 1798, Rome fell to the Invader."

"On June 3rd, 1798 the French Military Governor ordered that 30 Churches in Rome be leveled "for strategic reasons!" Among those Churches was St. Matthew's, which was the Shrine for the Icon of the 'Mother of Perpetual Help.' St. Matthew's was leveled, but the Icon was saved by Augustinian Monks who took it to an old Monastery to safekeep it there."

---

*Author's Note: (The information about the Churches in Rome was taken from the Roman Catholic Magazine *"Divine Love,"* issue No. 35, Volume 9, No. 2, Spring issue. I quoted from this Magazine because of the reported moving of the eyes, as witnessed at St. Paul's Cathedral in Hempstead, N.Y., March 23, 1960).

Extensively we shall learn of the *"Mother of Perpetual Help"* Icon when we describe the third Weeping Madonna. (p. 136).

Arrival in Washington

Finally, we were on our way to our Nation's Capital. During the long trip, we could not get over what we all had just witnessed only a short time ago.

In the silence of the night and the monotonous droning of our car, we spoke about the events of the Icon, and what a moving experience it had been for all, who took the time to come and be blessed by this *"Sign."*

We arrived at the Mayflower Hotel in Washington about midnight. The next morning we went to the Capitol to meet Senator Keating, only to be informed that the Senate had canceled the session of that morning.

I was very disappointed and somewhat frustrated after all the pressure and the agonizing I had gone through preceding our trip. However, the gracious Senator was very hospitable. We spent a relaxed hour in his office, and of course the subject of the *"Weeping Madonna"* came up.

The Senator had read the articles in the Washington Newspapers, but was interested to hear the facts first hand. I could tell that his interest was genuine, and this pleased me very much.

Fr. George Papadeas relating some of the facts
of the first Weeping Icon to Vice President Richard Nixon
while Senator Kenneth Keating listens.

During our visit with the Senator, he told us that together we would be visiting Vice President Richard Nixon in his office. The boys were really thrilled that they were going to meet the second in command of our Government.

Mr. Nixon was interested to hear the story of the *"Weeping Madonna"* and listened intently asking questions about the Icon.

It was a very warm and interesting visit. Our sons were elated to have received Mr. Nixon's autograph.

Having left the Vice President's Office, Senator Keating gave us a personal tour of the Capitol. He gave us much of the historical background of our governmental Offices, about which we were unfamiliar. I was thankful — especially that my two sons were so enriched, to have seen and heard the various historical aspects of our Capitol, and to have met so many Officials of our Government.

After the tour, we were honored by a Luncheon in the Vandenberg Room. By this time we felt like dignitaries, walking into that spacious ornate Vandenberg room to have lunch with so many distinguished Senators, like the late Senators Dirksen from Illinois, Leverett Saltonstall from Massachusetts, Styles Bridges from New Hampshire, and others.

After finishing our lunch, Senator Keating extended to us warm words of welcome.

He mentioned that while he was showing us around the Capitol he had interesting conversations with my sons.

With glowing phraseology he first introduced Dean to say a few words. Both our boys had worn their new three piece tweed suits, fittingly dressed for the occasion.

Everyone, including myself, was surprised when Dean got up with so much confidence to offer a few words before this august body.

Confidently pulling down on his vest, Dean took a stance, and after having properly addressed the Senators, he commenced to express the great honor he felt — how proud he was to be an American, etc.

His short meaningful patriotic remarks were greeted with warm applause. When Senator Keating asked Elias to offer a few words, he, not being as spontaneous as Dean laconically said: *"I am in full agreement with what my brother Dean said."* Commenting, Senator Keating said: "Elias, don't worry; with that smile, you can go anywhere and win people over!"

I then took the opportunity to thank Senator Keating and all the other Senators for the honored invitation and Luncheon, which will always remain a very memorable event in our life, even though I regret having missed the opportunity of invoking the Senate Prayer.

Because of previous commitments, I was compelled to return to our home base that same night. Before departing we did take advantage of the daylight hours to see some of the sites of our Nations Capital.

About 7:00 p.m. we were on our way home to Hempstead. It wasn't very difficult for my two sons to fall asleep on the back seat soon after such a long and eventful day.

The Return trip from Washington to Long Island

About midnight we were about to exit from the New Jersey Turnpike when we heard over the Radio: *"A breaking news story: a flash fire has completely gutted the St. Anthony's Shrine in Oceanside!"*

It really was very shocking news, because it was only a few days ago that I had met the Priest from the Shrine in the upstairs Catsounis apartment, when I had gone to see the tearing Icon.

It was very sad to hear the news of the devastating fire of the famous Shrine.

The long drive home felt like it was never ending at that late hour. My heart though, was filled with thanksgiving for the many things, which had transpired in this very concentrated period of my ministry.

✳

Home again

Lent was just about over. Our St. Paul's Parish would be preparing for Palm Sunday and the Holy Week Period. Besides our Members, who filled the pews in the two Divine Liturgies we celebrated every Sunday, we always had an additional steady influx of fellow Orthodox from many Metropolitan New York Parishes. If our Parish had been a busy one prior to March 16th, which it really was, one can well imagine the extra demands shouldered by us as a result of the *Miraculous Icon.*

Every day, from morning until nightfall we constantly came in contact with so many people from all over the Country. We were always happy to greet the many visitors and converse with them, even though there were schedules which had to be met, especially since Holy Week was upon us.

Palm Sunday over the years at St. Paul's was always exceedingly well attended. On that Holy Day we celebrated a third Liturgy to accommodate the many worshippers. In the three Divine Liturgies of Palm Sunday, 1960, including our parishioners, it was estimated that well over 5,000 were blessed, and had received a cross made from a palm frond given by one of the Priests.

In the Orthodox Church, Holy Week officially commences with the *"Nymphios"* (Bridegroom) Service on Palm Sunday evening. The sanctity and the solemnity of Holy Week is deeply felt when we see the Holy Altar, and the various fixtures in the Church covered and draped with black.

✻

The Second Tearing Icon
The "Portaitissa"

The date was April 12, 1960, Holy Tuesday, about noon. I was told by the Secretary, that a woman was hysterical over the phone and wanted to speak to me regarding an Icon of the Holy Mother tearing profusely. I picked up the phone and spoke to Mrs. Antonia Koulis of Oceanside trying to calm her in her excitement. She pleaded with me to come as soon as I could, because hundreds of people were already converging at her house.

Coincidentally, Mrs. Koulis was an aunt of Pagona Catsounis, who had given the first tearing Icon to St. Paul's.

I wasted no time. Quickly I summoned John Paul, the President of our Parish Council, to see if he was interested in joining me. Not only was he eager to come, but he also told me that this time he was going to bring a ledger to ask people to sign their names in testimony, if in fact they had seen the tears. This did not happen with the Catsounis' Icon, because everything happened so rapidly that we were totally unprepared.

I was, to put it mildly, very curious and anxious to see this second Weeping Icon. My mind was constantly revolving around so many thoughts which flashed across my mind regarding the *"Divine Signs."*

Without question I firmly believed, and believe that they were *Miraculous Signs.* In my heart and mind there was no question that these *"Signs"* were by Divine intervention. *"But, what could all this mean?"* That question kept rolling in my mind.

First in Island Park. Now, less than one month later in neighboring Oceanside at the home of Pagona Catsounis' aunt Mrs. Antonia Koulis, just minutes away from one another.

When the Catsounis couple had arrived from Greece, they had moved to Island Park, in order to be near their uncle and aunt Mr. & Mrs. Peter Koulis, who could give them guidance for their new beginning in America.

Approaching the Koulis' residence I wasn't surprised to see the hundreds of people already gathered near the house, and a steady stream ascending the outside wooden staircase which led to the second floor apartment.

It was almost a month ago that I had experienced a similar gathering and flow outside the Catsounis home.

Upon arrival we were greeted by Mrs. Antonia Koulis, who was visibly shaken. She led us to the *"Family Altar"* to see the Icon, an 8x10 lithographed Icon of the *"All-Holy Mother holding the Christ Child."*

The original *Miraculous Icon* of this lithographed print is in the Iveron Orthodox Monastery, dedicated to the *"Dormition of the Theotokos."* This Monastery is one of the 20 large Monasteries located on the renowned Mount Athos.

These massive, imposing Structures on a peninsula in northern Greece were built centuries ago to accommodate many thousands of Monks.

The *Miraculous Icon* of Iveron is known as the *"Panagia Portaitissa,"* (Greek, meaning *"All Holy Mother of the Portals or Gate.)"*

Approaching to venerate the *"Portaitissa"* Icon, I felt chills up my spine seeing, as from any live person, tears forming in both eyes of the lithographed print and freely rolling down the *"All-Holy Mother's "* cheeks onto Her garment and down to the base of the framed Icon. In flowing, the tears had formed two distinct and very visible wet tracks.

After praying the *"Paraklesis"* Service, I was besieged by the Reporters of all the major Metropolitan New York Newspapers.

They had already been interviewing some of the people who had come to view the Holy Icon.

Unexpectedly, after a few questions, I was asked by the Reporters if I would remove the lithographed Icon from the glass frame to inspect the back of the print. They wanted to ascertain the source of the fluid, if there was one. I responded that I would not do anything before calling His Eminence Archbishop Iakovos in New York City, which I was about to do anyway to inform him of this new *"Sign."*

I called His Eminence to inform him of this new *Manifestation.* He was totally surprised to hear of this second *"Sign"* and told me that he would not be able to come to Oceanside until after the *"Bridegroom"* Service of that evening at the Church of the Assumption in Brooklyn.

Relating certain things to the Archbishop regarding this second Weeping Icon, I told him that the N.Y. Reporters were asking me to remove the lithographed Icon from the glassed frame to inspect the back of the print. His Eminence quickly responded, *"under no circumstances; whoever wants to believe, let it be so."*

But, insistently I emphasized to him that we were not in Greece, where the population is almost 100% Orthodox, and where similar *"Signs"* have been witnessed, and Shrines have been built. I further said that this is a first, and indeed an almost inconceivable experience for the American scene.

Also the fact, that we were comparatively a minority Group among the plethora of Christian Bodies, and we should not leave any probable doubts in the minds of the people. We should be open to all and not fear the truth. If we did not permit the removal of the print to inspect the back of it, who knows how it would have been reported.

His Eminence finally conceded, but with absolute instructions, that no other hands except mine were to handle the Icon. The Reporters were very pleased that their request would be honored.

The lithographed print of the *"Panagia Portaitissa"* Icon which commenced tearing on April 12, 1960 in the home of Mr. & Mrs. Peter Koulis. It shed tears for almost 6 weeks.

With every possible reverence, and with awe, I turned the frame about, loosened a couple of fastenings and slowly pulled out the Icon from the frame.

I was amazed to see the inside face of the glass showing the same tracks of tears, rolling down to the base of the frame as were seen on the Icon behind this glass.

Much to everyone's surprise, including my own, the back of the print was bone dry.

The Reporters stood in awe, not uttering a word. They shook their heads, looking at one another with amazement. This was a first for all of them, in the many years of their careers. Understandably, their work must have brought them before unbelievable situations. But tears, emanating and continually flowing from the eyes of a lithographed print? Their silence was deafening. One could see that they were awed.

Now it would be next for them to question, *"why? What does it all mean?"* Very natural questions indeed.

After the *"Paraklesis"* in the Koulis home, Fr. George Papadeas holds the *"Portaitissa"* Holy Icon for Mrs. Antonia Koulis and Mrs. Pagona Parlamas to kiss it. (Mrs. Parlamas is Pagona Catsounis' Grandmother).

The visitors kept replenishing the long line, waiting patiently much beyond the Koulis house. John Paul, the Parish Council President with some assistance was busy asking people if they chose to sign the ledger after having seen the tears of the Icon. By early evening he had gathered over 2000 signatures for the Church's archives.

I was at the Koulis' home from early morning on Tuesday, until after 11:00 p.m. when His Eminence arrived with his entourage from the Brooklyn Church.

My day was spent conversing with Reporters, the Koulis family, some Parishioners of St. Paul's and many of the visitors, who had waited so patiently to view the Icon.

When His Eminence arrived, he was escorted to the *"Family Altar."* He stood silently before the Icon.

His amazement was noticeable while viewing a *Phenomenon,* which he had never experienced.

This was significant, because he did not arrive in time to see the tears of the first Icon. After a brief period of silence he held a Prayer Service, made the sign of the cross, and kissed the Icon. Preparing to depart, he announced that the Icon would be taken to St. Paul's on April 14th, Holy Thursday afternoon.

Shortly before midnight he departed, as we all

After the *"Paraklesis"* Archbishop Iakovos venerates the Holy Icon of the *"Portaitissa."*

did, to end the long spiritually eventful day.

The next day, Holy Wednesday, I celebrated the scheduled Pre-Sanctified Liturgy the last of the Lenten season.

In the evening I would be officiating at the Sacrament of the Holy Unction. I did make time though, that same afternoon to go and visit the Koulis home again.

When I arrived, I saw the endless line of people — not getting any shorter — patiently waiting for their turn to see the Icon. After approximately three hours at the Koulis home, I returned to St. Paul's to conduct the Holy Wednesday evening Holy Unction Service.

As requested by His Eminence, the schedule was to bring the Holy Icon from Oceanside to the Church on Holy Thursday in the afternoon.

On Holy Thursday morning, the Divine Liturgy of this very Holy Day has added significance for the Orthodox, because it is the celebration of the **Last Supper**, during which the Lord instituted the **Sacrament of the Holy Eucharist.**

It is this very Sacrament, which is celebrated worldwide by the Holy Orthodox Church during every Divine Liturgy of the year.

We may remember from the St. Matthew's Gospel, that the Lord, shortly before the Passion took the bread, and having given thanks, He broke it and gave to His Disciples saying: **"Take, eat; this is my Body;"** and taking the cup He offered thanks and gave to His Disciples saying: **"Drink from it, all of you, for this is my Blood of the New Testament, which is shed for many, for the remission of sins."** (Matthew 26:26-28). **"Do this in remembrance of Me."** (Luke 22:19)

This same gathering of the Lord and His Apostles at the **Last Supper** is repeated in every Divine Liturgy of the Orthodox Church. The most precious and crucial point of the Liturgy is during the *"Epiklesis"* (Greek for *'Invocation'*). At this moment the Priest prays for the Holy Spirit to descend and transform the bread and wine into the Body and Blood of the Lord.

Thus, by means of the Sacrament of the Holy Eucharist we are vividly brought back, and bonded to the Event of the Last Supper, by receiving our Lord's Body and Blood, as He desired for us to do, in order that we would be united with, and in Him.

While the faithful do receive Holy Communion during the regular Sunday Liturgies or on any of the weekday Liturgies, somehow, there is a feeling of deeper significance, as mentioned, for the Faithful to receive on Holy Thursday Morning.

There is the feeling, that we are closer to the Great Event of that Day; the **Last Supper,** which the Holy Orthodox Church, by the Lord's admonition, has been perpetuating for 2,000 years by celebrating the Sacrament of the Holy Eucharist, — and of course will continue to do so, until the second coming of our Lord, as the Great Judge!

This particular Holy Thursday, April 14, 1960, which had dawned, aside from being another beautiful Spring day, was very different from all the other ones we had ever experienced. It would forever be remembered, because of the added Event of bringing the second Tearing Icon to be enshrined in St. Paul's, in Hempstead, Long Island.

I recall so vividly my feelings of the vibrant spiritual exuberance felt on that Day by so many. I had just celebrated the *"unique"* Liturgy, and now in anticipation I was preparing for the exciting trip to Oceanside, and the enshrining of the second Holy Icon in our Church. The Congregation, as usual, had gathered after the Holy Thursday morning Liturgy in the spacious Hall for the Fellowship Hour, and all were eager to go to Oceanside to become a part of the historic motorcade.

I had requested the Nassau County Police Department to provide a motorcycle escort because of the large number of vehicles that would be taking part in the motorcade.

There were more than a few Policemen on motorcycles, some edging ahead to stop all the east-west traffic, and others continuing to lead us non-stop to Oceanside, and then to return to the Church with the Holy Icon.

I could see that His Eminence was very pleased with the spiritual excitement generated by the Event, and in which he had found himself participating. He expressed this pleasure to me as we traveled to Oceanside.

Having reached the Koulis' home we went directly before the Holy Icon to hold a brief Service, after which we would be returning to St. Paul's Cathedral for the enshrining with His Eminence officiating.

It is impossible to describe the massive, unforeseen turnout of our Parishioners for the return trip. Every street in that whole area was congested with automobiles leaving no open lanes for traffic. I never expected such a turnout!

Gradually our limousine got under way preceded by the Police escort with their lights flashing, and their sirens sounding, blocking all the east-west Long Island traffic until the last car had passed.

His Eminence Archbishop Iakovos and I, holding the Holy Icon, were the only occupants of the limousine following the Police escort. There was a count of 357 cars, which followed in the motorcade. In fact, I had read that it was the second largest motorcade in the history of Nassau County.

The first was, when President Eisenhower had visited Nassau County.

Arriving at the Church, we saw a battery of television cameras on tripods of the New York area T.V. Stations, and the multitudes around the Church.

It was a sight to behold! More importantly, one could sense the deep spiritual feeling that permeated the innermost

On the walkway to enter the Church Archbishop Iakovos holds the Holy
Icon escorted by Fr. George Papadeas to his left, Archdeacon Philip to
his right and Fr. Milton Efthimiou in foreground censing the Icon.
Antonia Koulis and Pagona Catsounis are close behind.

chamber of our hearts, and readily feel the calm and the
peace reflected in people's faces, which appeared to be contagious.

Viewing this serene environment I thought to myself —
Heaven would truly be on earth if this feeling could be trans-
mitted and maintained in all the world. It felt like all the
worldly affairs and cares, which routinely occupy our being,
were non-existent. Our hearts had been overwhelmed and
enveloped in this Great Event.

The Altar Boys lead the procession of the Choir, Clergy and Archbishop down the center aisle.

Everyone seemed to be virtually showered with the warmest feelings of love. This is the spiritual ecstasy that is felt, when our spiritual counterpart is given precedence, and predominates in our life!

His Eminence officiated at the *"Paraklesis"* Service, with over 40 Priests from the New York area participating.

There was a rampant spiritual exuberance deeply felt; — a feeling, which projected a distinctive solemnity, readily reflected on the countenances of the Congregation.

After venerating the two Icons, the second of which was tearing continuously, the faithful departed for home to

The Clergy facing the Holy Icons, while Archbishop Iakovos officiates at the enshrining of the *"Portaitissa"* Icon.
James Pappas directs the Choir on the Choir loft.

prepare for their return again to attend the three hour Holy Passion Service that evening.

During the Holy Thursday night Service the 12 Gospel excerpts are read pertaining to the Holy Passion.

Early on Great Friday the Royal Hours Service are read. In the afternoon, during the Great Friday Great Vespers Service, the Lord's Body is taken down from the Cross for the Funeral procession and the Entombment. It is a veritable re-enactment of the Biblical narrative, with a profound psychological impact, easily moving the faithful to tears.

In the evening of Great Friday, the Lamentation Service as always is very emotional. The flower-bedecked Sepulchre is placed in the area in front of the *"Iconostasis"* around which the Altar Boys, the Choir and the Clergy together with the Congregation sing the Lamentations .

The Holy Saturday morning Vespers, followed by the Divine Liturgy, herald the Midnight Paschal Resurrection Services. Conforming to the faithful adherence of the most ancient practices of the Church, the Eastern Orthodox Churches have kept very much alive the form of the most ancient Service of the Resurrection, which is not only symbolic, but spiritually exhilarating!

At the Midnight Resurrection Service one deeply feels the Lord's Resurrection, and most vividly!

One minute after Midnight the Church is completely darkened. All lights and candles are out. Not a single light, nor a lighted candle remains lit in the completely darkened Church, symbolizing the darkness of the Tomb. The only flickering flame seen, is from the Eternal Vigil Lamp on the Holy Altar. The Priest lights his candle from this Vigil Lamp and turning to face the Congregation holding the candle high chants:

"Come, receive the light from the Light which never wanes, and glorify Christ, Who has risen from the dead."

The Choir repeats this hymn as the Priest transmits the flame to the Altar Boys, who in turn walk down the aisle lighting the tapers held by the Congregation.

Gradually the light is spread throughout the Church, now completely illumined by candlelight, completely dispelling the darkness, thereby transmitting a superbly mystical feeling!

Preparing for the procession to exit from the Church to signify the empty Tomb, the Choir sings the hymn:

"The Angels of Heaven praise Your Resurrection O Christ, our Saviour; grant, that we here on earth may glorify You with a clean heart."

The Tomb that contained the Life of all is now empty. To symbolize the empty Tomb, the Church is vacated completely, led by the Choir, the Altar Boys, the Clergy and followed by the Congregation to the outside of the Church.

On a raised platform the Priest reads the Gospel of the Resurrection (Mark 16:1-8). Finishing the reading the Priest exclaims:

"Glory to the Holy, Consubstantial, Life-Giving and Undivided Trinity, now and ever, and to the Ages of Ages.

Taking the censer, the Priest commences to cense the Congregation, and with the candle held high in his left hand he leads the singing of the ever-glorious Hymn of the Resurrection:

"Christ has risen from the dead, by death trampling on Death, and bestowing life to those in the tombs."

After the Resurrection hymn is chanted repeatedly, everyone re-enters the Church for the Paschal Liturgy.

At the end of the Liturgy, the Priest hands each Member of the Congregation a dyed red egg wrapped in tulle declaring: **"Christ is risen!"** to which each Member responds: **"Truly, He is risen!"**

In the Orthodox tradition this mutual greeting replaces the everyday customary greeting for 40 days until the Ascension of the Lord.

The red-dyed Easter egg symbolizes the Blood of the Lord, through which the sins of mankind are washed away.

The egg, as we know, contains life. After the Resurrection Service the great Fast is now ended. The Members amongst themselves, breaking the strict fast, proceed to crack eggs with one another, repeating the Paschal greeting. By cracking the eggs, symbolically life springs forth, as did the Lord from the Grave! Consuming the egg, the faithful break their long fasting.

The Services of the Eventful Holy Week at St. Paul's culminated with the Easter afternoon Vespers on April 17, 1960. In this Service, the post-Resurrection Gospel (John 20:19-25) was read in various languages to signify the universality of the Christian Faith.

All the lengthy, but soul-stirring Services of Holy Week-Easter were over-subscribed at St. Paul's, — not only by our Parishioners but by the many Visitors.

The spiritual impact of the tearing Icons, had been deeply felt by the Orthodox, as well as countless people of all Faiths, who came St. Paul's in droves to partake of the spiritual fulfillment.

It was now Monday morning, the day after the Glorious Easter Day. Visitors had already formed a line.

They had come early. It was estimated that between 8,000-10,000 daily waited patiently for their turn to come before the Icons to sense the blessing. The line outside the Church was blocks long.

It was a very moving sight to watch the endless line of visitors standing in an orderly manner, each one anxiously awaiting their turn. One could easily sense the religious aura

Typical of the lines that formed every day , waiting ever so patiently
to enter the Church to revere the Holy Icons.

that dominated the whole scene. The Reporters, who had set
up camp at St. Paul's had noted and remarked about this.

At intervals, during the day and night I would leave
my office and walk into Church through the entrance at the
south transept, which connects the Church proper to the
Administration Building.

I made myself available to many people, who would
approach me, to either ask for some detail about the Icons, or
to reveal something confidential, which had been heavily
weighing on their soul.

They strongly felt, that this was a God-given opportunity to unburden themselves. It was like having a portable
confessional.

Frankly commenting, the spiritual fulfillment was
great for so many people, as it was for me, in witnessing the
expression of relief they reflected after their unburdening.

The Icons provided so many positive and uplifting
experiences, one after another, — some known and most not!

At times, I would stand in some corner of the Church unobserved, to watch the people approaching to venerate the Icons. Most of them appeared to me to be within the realm of an identical religious aura. This sight was enough to convince anyone that all humans do indeed have the same basic feelings of love and devotion; — and why shouldn't they? Aren't we all the children of God, — brothers and sisters?

The unfortunate thing is, that for so many this spiritual euphoria is not of a lasting nature, because people permit themselves to get enveloped so easily, and literally be overcome by the necessities, the cares and the abundance of this world. This can be understood by the Lord's *"Parable of the Sower."* (p. 41).

God bestowed upon all humans a free will. The choices of using this free will are strictly ours. People can allow themselves to become hardened, or they conversely can choose to keep their hearts warm, mellow and alert to the needs of others.

I believe, that if any came before the Holy Icons with hardened hearts, they must have felt their hearts mellow simply by standing in line, and then approaching before the Holy Icons to offer their prayers, even if this may have been for them a momentary emotional experience.

To be sure, the beauty of the St. Paul's Cathedral, with its wealth of Iconography may have contributed some spiritual feeling to many, who were not acquainted with the Orthodox Church. It could have possibly given them a deeper feeling for their faith.

In anticipation, — waiting in those endless lines for hours, they must have believed, that they were about to come in contact with something unbelievable to be sure, — inexplicable, and soul-stirring, unlike anything they had experienced.

It was very touching for me, as I witnessed many people walking away from the Icons with tears of their own, after having seen the tears of the second Icon. This Icon's continuous tearing lasted for almost six weeks, day and night. At times we held all-night Vigils as is done in the Monasteries.

A few of the visitors also offered their *"Tamma"* (Greek word for "vow," promise, or offering), leaving their personal sentimental gift of a ring, a cross, a pendant, a piece of jewelry, etc. on the Icon, all of which were secured on a ribbon, strung in front of the second Icon.

Among these *"Tammata"* (Plural of *"Tamma)"* there were also Stars of David with silver chains. This was also very moving, — and a proof, that the religious feeling is a common thread that binds all people, regardless of affiliation.

Seeing the Stars of David showed, that even people of the Hebrew Faith* had come to offer their prayers before the Icons. (* see p.39 for relative reference by a Reporter of the **WORLD TELEGRAM and SUN).**

These *"tammata"* would one day be used for the future Shrine to be dedicated to the *"Theotokos."*

My involvement with the endless lines of *"pilgrims"* had become an everyday affair lasting on into the night. I must say, that I thoroughly enjoyed meeting and talking with the people from all walks of life.

My Parish duties had become transformed to *"ecumenical."* In order that I could have the necessary freedom and the time to concentrate on all aspects which pertained to the Holy Icons, I relegated most of the many Parish duties to my two beloved colleagues, Frs. Milton Efthimiou and George Kambanis.

Our phones rang incessantly with inquirers asking about the Icons and directions to get to St. Paul's.

We welcomed a total of 111 organized Pilgrimages within 3 months, which are on record. These consisted of at least one, and often two, three and four Buses bringing the faithful from our Orthodox Parishes from points as far west as Chicago, as well as from all parts of the East Coast.

Fr. George Papadeas often spoke after the *"Paraklesis"* Services held for the pilgrims, who had come from afar.

On a daily basis these Pilgrimages led by their respective Priests would gather near the Icons and chant the *"Paraklesis"* Service. I was so very happy to pray with the Priests and their Congregations.

It was a special delight for me to welcome the many thousands converging at St. Paul's, to partake in drinking from the same *"spiritual fountain,"* from which we all had been so refreshed. It was for all a most uplifting experience.

Students from the many Metropolitan New York area schools escorted by their Teachers, came to view and pray before the Icons.

They stood reverently in line for their turn to see and venerate the Holy Icons.

As previously noted, the Reporters from the Metropolitan New York City Newspapers had encamped at St. Paul's, and daily they interviewed and mingled with many, who had filed before the Holy Icons.

The front page of the afternoon edition of the **NEW YORK JOURNAL AMERICAN** on April 13, 1960, showed a large photograph of the tearing Icon in the Koulis home taken by their Staff photographer, Max Finklestein.

Students with their Teachers from the Greek Cathedral Parochial School came to revere the Holy Icons. Fr. Milton Efthimiou welcomed the Teachers and Pupils.

The picture published on the front page of that paper showed very clearly the tears streaming from the eyes of the Holy Mother.

By coincidence, the Editor of **The JOURNAL AMERICAN** George Carpozi Jr. was a subscribing Member of our St. Paul's Orthodox Church in Hempstead.

He personally called to tell me that Mel Finklestein dashed into the newsroom brimming with excitement and enthusiastically declared something to the effect that, *"I don't know about you people. Although I am of the Jewish Faith, I absolutely believe in what I saw and photographed!"*

Coincidentally, in preparing to write this Book, I had sent a brief questionnaire to 20 of my Friends and former Parishioners of St. Paul's, asking them to express their sentiments and opinions of their 1960 experience, and now, 40 years later what their feelings are. Some of these will be quoted toward the end of this Book. But, having just mentioned about Mel Finklestein, one of my Parishioner-Friends in the questionnaire returned to me stated that she saw Mr. Finklestein kneel when the Holy Icon was brought in procession to St. Paul's.

She later had the opportunity to speak to him, and he related to her that this *Miraculous Event* had brought him back to his Religion. How powerful indeed is the spiritual re-awakening and the religious motivation! God be praised for His Marvelous Works!

To my estimation, this and other similar expressions and admissions are what constitute miracles in life.

It is so gratifying to see people spiritually energized. Miracles are a true and positive force in our Society.

As mentioned, when people speak of miracles, they automatically lean toward the physical healing. We somehow tend to by-pass the *"miracles"* which transform people's souls! I feel confident and believe, that every day all around the world among all the races, colors and creeds, the *"miracles"* within the soul are happening at all times.

These *"miracles"* are not recorded, but they are surely responsible for many of the wonderful things happening in this life.

In the April 18, 1960 edition of the **WORLD TELEGRAM and SUN,** Dave Balch, a Staff writer, mentioned in his article a few of the comments which had been made to him: "A mother speaking to her two small children said: 'We have seen a miracle.'

An elderly woman to a younger one: *'It's an Easter Sign to the whole world!'* One man to another: *'I didn't think I could believe it, but I do'.*"

Continuing, Dave Balch wrote: "Some of those passing the Madonna brushed the simple frame lightly with their fingers, as their lips moved in prayer. Others kissed the glass covering the lithograph of the Mother and Child. As some worshippers gazed at it, their own eyes filled with tears."

"The eyes of the Madonna have not been dry since last Tuesday, when the tear-like flow was first observed by Mrs. Peter Koulis of Oceanside."

In the April 19, 1960 edition of the same Newspaper, among other things, Dan Foley wrote: *"Some 500 an hour, the pilgrims filed into St. Paul's Greek Orthodox Cathedral on Cathedral Avenue, Hempstead, L.I., until a late hour last night."*

"And today they come. Clutching rosaries, or murmuring prayers, or trying to quiet babes-in-arms in the hush of the Church, they advance to where two Icons of the Madonna are enshrined before the Altar for veneration."

"Here is a man by himself, on his way home from work. There is a family of four — and some children on Easter vacation. In one of the pews are two Roman Catholic Nuns, fingering their rosary beads in prayer."

"There were approximately 5,000 visitors yesterday — representing all Creeds — and many more were expected today, before the Church is finally closed for the night. They all hope to see the tears in the Madonna's eyes. They kiss the Icons, and lift up youngsters to kiss them. Or they touch the images and make the Sign of the Cross."

"There were many testimonials to the weeping of the Oceanside Icon. Said M..... R......, of Lynbrook, L.I., 'It's miraculous. It's unbelievable!' Observed Mrs. S..... S...., of Massapequa, L.I., who visited the Shrine with her three young boys: 'I saw tears glistening in the corners of the eyes'." "Another observer described the tears as 'glistening like diamonds'."

"The two Catholic Nuns, who visited the Hempstead Church said they were teachers and that they had a number of Greek Orthodox children in their classes. They said they were saying their beads for the intention that the Roman Catholic and Orthodox Churches might be reunited."

"Why was the Madonna weeping? Did it indicate sadness or something else? The two Nuns thought it was some sign — perhaps relating to the intention for which they were praying."

"No one seemed to have a clear idea of why the Madonna should be weeping, but 'I've never seen anything like it,' the people chorused. Says Fr. George, the Hempstead Pastor: 'What mother does not cry for her children, when she sees her son or daughter straying'!"

"The first weeping Icon was for the believers. The second Icon was for the skeptics. This might mean the return for many to salvation....'."

Another Reporter, Mr. Martin Steadman wrote a two column article captioned: **"REPORTER'S OWN STORY OF L.I. PICTURE,"** with the sub-caption: *"I definitely saw the Madonna's Tears."*

Mr. Steadman wrote: *"I saw tears in the eyes of the Madonna. I've been a Reporter for five years, and I have the newspaperman's almost habitual skepticism. But, notwithstanding laboratory and chemical tests claiming that the Madonna of Oceanside's tears are not real, I know that without any shadow of doubt I saw tears in the eyes."*

"I had gone to St. Paul's Greek Orthodox Church, at 110 Cathedral Ave., Hempstead, L.I., to see for myself."

"The Madonna I speak of, is the colored lithograph that last Tuesday afternoon began to weep in the home of Mr. and Mrs. Peter Koulis of 2822 Oceanside Rd., Oceanside, L.I.

On Holy Thursday the picture of the Blessed Virgin was taken in a motor procession to the Church."

"I arrived at the Church soon after the Good Friday Services had concluded. Other Reporters informed me that the Madonna had shed six tears during the Mass."

"There was a line of people slowly moving forward to where the Madonna was, just to the left of the Altar. The Madonna was in a glass enclosed frame and surrounded by Easter lilies. Near it was another Madonna that had wept

from the left eye March 16 in the home of Mrs. Koulis' niece, Mrs. Pagona Catsounis of 41 Norfolk Rd., Island Park, L.I.

Both pictures were atop wooden stands on the marble Altar. The picture of the Virgin that had wept in the Catsounis home has not shed tears since soon after it first had wept."

"When I looked at the second one, at first I did not see tears. But when I moved closer, to almost within an inch of the predominantly gold and red colored lithograph, I saw them.

In the left eye, in the corner near the nose, two tiny beads of moisture glistened from the lights of the brightly illuminated Byzantine-style Church."

"In the right eye, near the corner, was a single gleaming tear. The eyes of the Madonna are roughly half the size of an adult's, and all the tears were in exact proportion to the eyes."

"The picture, which had candles burning near it, was slanted backward at an angle of bout 30 degrees. I waited for the tears to roll down the cheeks, but they did not.

For several hours I remained at the Church, and in all that time the tears remained where I first had seen them.

What did I think when I actually saw what many have called a Phenomenon? My main thought was what the Church's Pastor, the Rev. George Papadeas had said: 'why did the tears form in the eyes, as they would from a living person, and not just anywhere else in the lithograph'? "

I am a Roman Catholic and have a sister who is a Nun and I can only wonder at what I have seen.

Sometime in the near future, Father Papadeas told me, a Shrine will be built for the two Icons of the "Weeping Madonna."

Inspiring and Energizing Faith

From among the many wonderful experiences I had talking with people about the Icons, I'll never forget a Physician of the Roman Catholic Faith.

He impressed me as a devout believer, after having met and conversed with him in my office.

He had already been in the Church and prayed before the Holy Icons as he later told me. He had requested to meet me since he had read my name in his City's Newspaper.

The Doctor had driven all night from Akron, Ohio accompanied by his devoted Mother. Presently, they were preparing for the long trip back to Akron, because of his professional obligations.

When he first came into my office, I asked him a question, which as a Priest I never should have: *"Doctor, did you see the tears?"*

In retrospect, I cannot believe, that I had asked such a superficial question.

Perhaps I was so caught up in this amazing Event, that I involuntarily shifted from the spiritual, having referred only to what our eyes could see.

It is then that I received one of the greatest lessons of my life by the Doctor's most powerful answer of true faith to my question. In instances such as this one, doesn't the Bible give us the answer when it states in (Psalm 8:2)?

"Out of the mouths of infants and nursing babes, You have established strength."

The Doctor responded: *"Father, I believe. — I did not drive all those hours by night from Akron to come to see the tears. I believe what has been testified by yourself and so many as I read in the repeated articles in our local Newspaper. I didn't come to see the tears."*

"My sole purpose was to come with my dear Mother to venerate before the Icon of our Holy Mother, and to ask for Her blessing in our life, because we firmly believe that She is the loving Mother of us all."

You can imagine how humbled I felt upon hearing this most profound confession of faith!

The Doctor's faith reminded me of the Lord's words to the Centurion, extolling his great faith. Matthew 8:5-13, to which I briefly refer.

The Centurion of the Roman Army was a pagan.

He had heard of the wondrous works of the *"Miracle Worker."* When one of his most devoted servants was seriously ailing, the Centurion, as the Roman Official of Capernaum, and having heard that Jesus had come into town, was overwhelmed by a strong feeling to plead with the *"Miracle Worker"* to effect the cure. With religious fervor he approached Jesus and appealed to Him to heal his servant.

The Lord was sympathetic and told him that he would come to his house to effect the cure; whereupon the Centurion said: *"I am not worthy for You to come under my roof. Just say the word only, and I believe that my servant will be healed."*

When the Lord heard these words of such strong faith He said: *"Verily, I have not found so great a faith; not even in Israel! Go your way, and as you have believed, so be it done."* And the servant of the Centurion was miraculously healed at that very hour.

I have never forgotten my shortcoming in this instance, as I surely have not forgotten how deeply the Doctor's profound faith and devotion had touched my heart.

The Doctor's faith also brought to my mind the verse from St. Paul's Epistle to the Hebrews, Chapter 11:1, in which he gives us a definition of *"faith."*

"Faith is the substance of things hoped for, — the evidence of things not seen."

As I have mentioned, I remember most vividly the many facts, which surrounded the mystery of the Holy Icons and the effect they have had on many people by their miraculous expression.

As has been mentioned, when we speak of miracles, we somehow think automatically in terms of the healing from some physical ailment. That is, for a paralytic to walk, a blind person to see, a deaf person to hear, etc

I repeat, that we should never lose sight of the healing of the soul, which is a major miracle. These *miracles* of soul-healings go unheralded for the most part, simply because of their relatively subjective and private matter.

My contact with many hundreds of people during those months of spiritually treasured experiences convinced me, that more than a few soul-healing *"miracles"* must have come to pass.

❊

Two Physical and Spiritual Healings which came to my attention

After the Service of the Royal Hours of Great Friday morning, a communicant from the St. Spyridon Greek Orthodox Church in upper Manhattan approached me to express his joy, and the thanksgiving he felt in his heart.

He said that he had experienced a complete fulfillment in his life after his first visit to pray before the Icons.

This was his second visit to the enshrined Icons. He came to offer his heartfelt gratitude. Although in his prayers at home he had repeatedly thanked God for the miracle, yet he wanted to make the pilgrimage to St. Paul's to express his gratitude to the Lord, through our *"Panagia,"* the loving Mother of us all.

He told me that for years he had suffered from a very severe case of eczema all over his body, and that he had spent tremendous amounts of money visiting many Doctors and purchasing medicines.

When the first news of the Tearing Icons came to his attention through the Newspaper articles, he decided to make the pilgrimage from Washington Heights to St. Paul's to pray before the Icon of the Blessed Mother.

From the very first moment he learned of the *"Divine Sign,"* he prayed fervently. Inwardly he had sensed an unusually strong feeling that he had never felt before. He firmly believed, that the Lord through His Holy Mother would hear his prayer and show His mercy on him, in that he had endured his ailment with patience for many years.

The Lord did hear his prayer. He related to me that he had been completely cured. While I do not remember his name, I can easily visualize seeing him standing before me —relating his joy and gratitude for his healing.

This was the first physical healing, of which I personally heard from the one who was healed.

During the post-Easter period, I had gone one morning to visit one of my very dear Parishioners in the Hospital.

When I returned, the Secretary of the Church informed me that a miracle had taken place shortly before I had returned to my office. She told me, as did the caretakers and the Nun of St. Paul's, Sister Thekla, that a Family from Chicago had come to pray before the Holy Icons.

The Secretary told me that she and others of the St. Paul's Staff heard what sounded like someone the firing of a gun in the Church. Having rushed into the Church, they saw a young girl jumping up and down screaming with joy. It was, they told me, a heart-rending scene to see this young girl in the arms of her Parents, hugging her tightly .

"I hear, I hear," she shrieked joyfully over and over again. She had heard human sounds for the first time, having been deaf since infancy.

The imagined *"gunshot"* heard by the Personnel was the very loud popping of a flash bulb, used in those days, after a picture of the Family was snapped near the Icons.

The popping of the flash bulb was greatly amplified by the reverberations bouncing off the arches and dome of the Cathedral and really sounded, as was said, like a gunshot.

The young girl's ears registered sounds precisely at the moment the flash bulb exploded, as she related to all present.

Of course a question may arise: *"Was it the exploding bulb that perhaps affected her eardrum in some manner, and as a result she had heard?"* or, *"was it an act of Grace of the Holy Mother, who through Her Son, our Lord Jesus, which effected the miracle?"* The answer to these questions can be supplied by each one of us, according to the measure of faith that we have.

Personally, and without any doubt, I believe that it was a supernatural act, which is classified as a true *Miracle!*

Regardless though, of how one chooses to believe, I was so very happy for that Family from Chicago. I envisioned the great joy upon their return to their City, completely fulfilled, and proclaiming their gift of faith; that is, the *Miracle* which happened when they prayed before the Icons of the Blessed Mother and Ever-Virgin Mary.

Archbishop requests Official Pronouncement from the Patriarch

Archbishop Iakovos, keeping current with the news regarding the Icons, as reported almost daily in the Metropolitan New York Papers, and having been asked for his evaluation, proclaimed repeatedly that he considered the *Manifestations* from *"Above"* as a *"True Sign"* that God was speaking to us.

Thus, he wrote to the Supreme Head of our Church, the Patriarch in Constantinople to render an Official pronouncement.

His Eminence's letter to the Patriarch was as follows:

Your All Holiness:

A sign appeared in the home of the devoted Peter Koulis Family. The Icon of the Holy Mother, a print of the miraculous Icon of the "Portaitissa" of the Iveron Holy Monastery on Mount Athos, has been continuously shedding tears.

Having visited the home personally, I saw what others had seen, and were seeing; that the Icon was tearing.

The awesome experience of tearing I ascertained also on Holy Wednesday.

On Holy Thursday, in a most impressive motorcade, we brought the tearing Holy Icon to the Saint Paul's Church.

The miracle was witnessed by thousands of our Orthodox Christians, as well as those of other Christian Denominations, as also of other Faiths, by young and old alike. Over two thousand have registered with their signatures that they were witnesses to the miracle.

The Archdiocese gave permission to the Newspaper Reporters not only to examine the Holy Icon, but also to receive a specimen of the tears for a laboratory chemical analysis. Until now the tearing continues without any doubt from anyone. Representatives of other Churches, people of a doubting nature, and even disbelievers, admitted that they saw the Icon of the Holy Mother tearing.

The Newspapers, the Radio and Television Stations,

the Movie Theaters brought to the whole of America the Miracle of the Panagia.

With my deepest respect.

+ Iakovos, Archbishop of America

The reply and official pronouncement of the Patriarchate was, that the *Manifestations* of the Weeping Icons of the *"Theotokos"* were declared as a *"Divine Sign."*

Without question, the *Supernatural Phenomenon* of the tearing Icons was universally accepted. So many may have been questioning, *"how could tears have possibly appeared on a lithographed print?"* But no such question was able to stand before the reality, as witnessed by countless thousands.

As mentioned, the second Icon of the Holy Mother of Iveron was removed from its frame at the request of the New York. Newspaper Reporters to verify from where the tears were emanating.

This was done, after receiving permission from the Archbishop to do so. Thus the New York Reporters, who wanted to see the back of the Icon were satisfied. Their amazement was evident, having seen that there was no source of tears, or moisture on the back of the lithographed Icon.

This was described by the **NEW YORK NEWSDAY** Reporter Jim Hadjin as perfectly dry of any liquid in the back after the Icon was removed from the frame. (see p. 69 and 170).

Laboratory Analysis of the Tears

There was no question that the tears on the Holy Icons had been universally seen, and accepted as such. Now there arose a new and unexpected development.

One morning I received a call from the Editor of the **WORLD TELEGRAM and SUN**, the afternoon Metropolitan New York Paper.

This popular Newspaper had fully covered the story of the Icon from the beginning, using very large type for its headlines and pictures on its front pages for five days.

The Editor was asking me for permission to have the tears analyzed by a New York Chemical Laboratory. I thought that the burden of proof had passed when we submitted to the previous request to remove the Icon from the frame, which revealed no visual source of the tears.

Hardly anyone could have ever imagined, or anticipated this newest request for permission to analyze the tears.

I could not give the Editor an answer, without consulting firstly with His Eminence the Archbishop.

I called His Eminence, and informed him of this new request. He was rather reticent, thinking that we might be going too far. I repeated that, which I originally said to him, when the Reporters had asked me to remove the Icon from the frame on the very first day of the tearing, April 12, 1960.

Again he conceded and told me to use my judgement with extreme care, which I would have done anyway.

The chemists commissioned by the **WORLD TELEGRAM and SUN** came with their syringes and took samples of the tears.

Two days later, the Editor called to tell me that the analysis was done by the New York Testing Laboratories, and that **"the tears were of an oily nature, which they couldn't classify among the known elements, and that the tears of the Icon had only a trace of chloride, a major element of human tears, and no nitrogenous compounds, usually found in tears."**

I responded with an expression of joy, after hearing the results of this analysis. I told him that I would never want to think and believe, that the Ever-Virgin Mary's tears of empathy and love were of the same substance as our frail human tears! I choose to believe, that the Holy Mother's tears surely possess therapeutic value for both body and soul!

I was also happy to have heard that the substance was *"oily."* The Laboratory did not know what type of oil, but that the tears were of *"an oily nature!"* Human tears are not oily in nature, but those of our All-Holy Mother were. That is why my response to the Editor of the **WORLD TELEGRAM** was, that I would have been somewhat disappointed, if I had heard that the tears of the *"Panagia"* were similar to our frail tears!

We do know, that in ancient times olive oil was extensively used, not only as an edible, but also as a type of therapeutic agent for soothing pain and healing.

Even today, when we read the specifications of the *"over the counter medicines"* for the relief of pain and therapy for the skin, we see that they contain some type of oil.

At this point, I did not gloss over the finding that the tears *"were of an oily nature, which they* (the chemists) *could not classify!"* This revelation deepened the mystery and brought forth the quality of God's mysterious and inexplicable expressions, which cannot be analyzed or deciphered by finite humans!

There is no question that faith in God, lacking very much in many people, must always come into play.

I was very happy that the Church responded fully to all the requests made by the New York Press, so that no questions had remained unanswered. The Church passed all the tests of scrutiny requested by the Press and the Professionals.

The analysis of the Tears was the final request of the publishing world, which was accordingly reported in the Newspapers.

For me, this newest certification of the inexplicable regarding the Icon, served to deepen the Mystery; — a Mystery, which always surrounds every true *Miracle*.

It is known, that the Media does seek to keep newsworthy stories alive. The Holy Icons were a case in point.

Without any doubt, all the Events of the Icons, which had served to bolster the faith of the people around the world, also sealed the mouths of many, who could be classified as disbelievers or disbelievers. The *"Divine Signs"* truly served to further open the hearts and minds of the believers.

The Reporters were still being kept busy asking professionals and other people for their opinions.

In a **NEW YORK NEWSDAY** report, dated April 13, 1960, Reporters Bill Butler and Dave Kahn reported among other things, as follows:

Oceanside — "Another Greek Orthodox Icon of the Virgin Mary shed tears yesterday. The phenomenon — the second reported on Long Island within a month — drew the immediate interest of scientists."

"Scores of observers — including four Newsday Staff Members — reported seeing tears well in the corner of the picture's eyes. The highest Greek Orthodox Prelate in the western hemisphere, Archbishop Iakovos, also witnessed the tears and pronounced the phenomenon a 'Divine sign,' as he had with the first Icon."

"Scientists, engineers, and art experts could offer no natural explanation for the phenomenon. The Chairman of Hofstra College's chemistry department, for example, said:

'I read of the first case. I could think of nothing at all that could explain that situation, and this of course is of the same nature'."

"The tears were first seen about noon yesterday by the owner of the Icon, Mrs. Antonia Koulis, 40, who is an aunt of Mrs. Pagona Catsounis, the owner of the first weeping Icon."

"I was frightened," Mrs. Koulis said. *"I couldn't move for five minutes."* But, she finally managed to awaken her husband, Peter, 56, a night cashier at a Diner. Like his wife, he was at first transfixed, when he saw the tears."

About 1:20 p.m., they asked their priest, the Rev. George Papadeas, to come to their home at 2832 Oceanside Rd..

"Fr. Papadeas, Pastor of St. Paul's Greek Orthodox Church of Hempstead, where the first Icon is installed in a special Shrine, carefully examined the framed 8 by 10 inch, multicolored lithograph titled *'Portaitissa.'* It stood on a shelf crowded with 19 other Icons in a second-story bedroom."

"Father Papadeas saw drops of a clear liquid well in the corners of the eyes of the *"Panagia,"* which appeared moist and swollen with dampness."

"More drops stood at intervals along wet streaks that ran down the front of the picture. At the bottom, the cardboard backing had soaked up some of the moisture. The picture was not wet elsewhere."

"As word of the *Phenomenon* spread through the neighborhood, visitors began streaming into the Koulis home.

Early today, when a devotional Service was conducted by four priests, the house was still filled with dozens of people. Of the scores who saw the tears, many left with radiant faces; all exclaimed over the *Phenomenon.* The witnesses included Greek Orthodox, Roman Catholic, Protestants and Jews."

"Among the witnesses were four Newsday Staff Members: reporters Jim Hadjin and Bill Butler and photographers Jim Nightingale and Dick Morseman".

"All four — who covered the event in relays — said they went to Oceanside in a skeptical frame of mind, not expecting to see anything. **But all four confirmed that they saw the tears.**"

"Morseman, who had not seen any tears in the first 'Weeping Icon' while taking pictures of it, said: *'I'm a skeptical guy — and I saw tears.'* Nightingale said, *'I didn't believe it. Now I don't know what to believe'.*"

"Scientists who were asked for an explanation frankly admitted they were baffled."

"Dr. Malcolm H. Preston of Douglaston, chairman of Hofstra's fine arts department, said: *'Though I cannot recall chapter and verse, I am sure that there are reports of phenomena like this. I have never seen any explanation that would satisfy everyone.*

I wouldn't rule out the possibility of condensation, but this would be relatively difficult. I know of nothing in painting that would cause this'."

"Anthony Giardina of Baldwin, president of the Nassau Chapter of the New York State Society of Professional Engineers, said: *'The one possibility was.....condensation. But from the engineering possibilities, I don't think you can explain it'.*"

"His predecessor, **Clifford J. Dvorak** of Bellmore, could suggest no natural explanation and said: *'There's a strong element of the spiritual there'.*"

"John Stamataky, a Bronx engineer who had viewed the first Icon, said that the repeated Phenomenon *'is beyond my powers to explain'.*"

"Dr. J. George Lutz of W. Hempstead, head of the Chemistry department of Hofstra University, tentatively advanced the theory that *'some pigment attracts water, a humectant* (moisturizing agent) *of sorts.'* — He then withdrew it, adding: *'But I wouldn't want to venture that'."*

"Dr. Harold E. Clearman of Hicksville, chairman of the College's physics department, declined even to suggest any theories."

"Caroline Keck of Brooklyn, a leading expert in the preservation of paintings, said pointedly: *'This isn't anything for a conservator. This is something for the religious'."*

"Dr.J.B. Rhine, head of the Parapsychology Laboratory of Duke University in North Carolina said: *'Something is going on there that is beyond the normal, the natural, the things we know.'* He urged further detailed study of the *'Phenomenon'."*

The above article, printed here in its entirety, showed that the Reporters wanted to be as thorough as possible in their reporting, and asked questions, not only from those waiting to see the icons, but from various professionals.

The Reporters' articles added greatly to the mystery of the *"Divine Sign,"* which simply and reverently was accepted by believing souls with the fulness of faith in their hearts.

Of course, the pundits of the scientific world, resourceful in their science and findings, base their conclusions on experimentation — on calculations, and a progression from one discovery to another.

However, it is interesting to note, that it was not only the above mentioned scientists or engineers, who made mention of moisture. This was heard many times and perhaps could have been applied to the Holy Icons, that is, if the *"moisture"* was emanating from the forehead, or the cheek, or garment, or hands, or the background, etc.

Moisture, of course can appear on any object. Without question though, the reality regarding the *"Divine Signs"* through the Holy Icons remains, **that it was not in the least a case of moisture, but actually of tears, resembling our human tears, emanating directly from the eyes, and not from any area on the face of the background of the Icons.** This was acknowledged and attested by the hundreds of thousands that viewed the Icon.

Then again we must never forget, that both the Catsounis and Koulis Families had over 15 Icons on their *"Family Altars."*

If there had been a case of moisture, which most assuredly was not the case, one could ask: *"why didn't this moisture appear on any part of the other Icons?"*

By no means can anyone expound the *"moisture"* theory, regarding the Holy Icons. It just does not stand.

The *Manifestation* of the tearing Icons, was without question precise and definitive.

Also, there is the item I have already mentioned, which adds further credence. The fact that the three Icons had different size faces as painted by the Iconographers of the original Icons, and that the size of the tears were in direct proportion to the eyes.

In comparable cases to the inexplicable Manifestations, there will always be those, who will continue to question and doubt, regardless of the consonance and irrefutable testimony of many others.

But, the loving heart, which believes that God, the Creator of the Universe Who is All-Powerful and Omniscient, can easily comprehend God's Omniscience by reading from the **20th to the 27th verse in the 1st Chapter of lst Corinthians, as stated by St. Paul:**

20. "Where is the wise person? where is the scribe? where is the debater of this world?

Has not God made foolish the wisdom of this world?
21. For since in the wisdom of God, the world through its wisdom did not come to know God, God was well pleased through the foolishness of preaching to save those, who believe."

And in this same chapter, St. Paul continues, verse *22.* *"Because the Jews ask for a sign, and the Greeks seek after wisdom, 23. but we preach Christ crucified, unto the Jews a stumbling block, and unto the Greeks foolishness;*
24. But unto them which are called, both Jews and Greeks, Christ is the power of God, and the wisdom of God. 25. Because, the foolishness of God is wiser than men; and the weakness of God is stronger than of men. 26. For you see your calling, brethren, that there are not many wise men according to the flesh, not many mighty, not many noble; 27. But God has chosen the foolish of the world to shame the wise; and the weak of the world to shame the strong."

Another simple, yet Inexplicable Phenomenon

Reminiscing the spiritual happenings at the time of the Weeping Madonna, I'll never forget one of my former Parishioners, Mrs. Angeliki Pittas of Island Park. Her Family lived in an apartment over their Restaurant.

One night the Building caught fire from a lightning of an electrical storm, which struck a transformer. As a result, their building was completely gutted. After a few days, Mrs. Pittas came into my office at St. Paul's with a picture of the Weeping Icon which she had cut out from a magazine and framed between two pieces of glass.

It was the only item they managed to salvage from the disastrous fire, after they had searched the charred rubble for any possible personal belongings. It was at the insistence of their 12 year-old daughter that they combed the charred rubble to see if they could find the Icon.

(Author's Note: 12 year old Anita Pittas had a strong feeling that she would be able to find her paper Icon framed between 2 pieces of glass. Although the building was gutted, she searched as with a fine tooth comb in the blackened rubble and found her Icon, bringing her indescribable joy. Indeed, another fact difficult to explain).

This was an added mystery, as insignificant as it may have appeared. How was it, that everything was completely burned and charred, except this partly burned paper Icon in a glass frame?   It was charred along the edges only up to the face and body of the *"All-Holy Mother,"* but the faces on the paper print were intact. This gift of Mrs. Pittas made to the Church at the time of the weeping, was unavailable at this writing.

I knew though, that she had moved to Florida's west Coast some years ago, and on occasion I would see and speak with her at Church functions. Recently, I called to remind her of the glass-framed Icon she had given St. Paul's 40 years ago.

I asked her if she had any photos of same to be included in this Book. She informed me, that she did have a picture, but that it was not a good reproduction.

She explained that it did show the charring up to the face of the Madonna. I asked her to send me a copy, if possible, and to describe briefly the devastation of the fire which I do remember. She did, and I thanked her.

This is what she wrote to me:

July. 27, 2000

Dear Father George:

It was good to hear your voice yesterday and a pleasure to hear that you are publishing a Book on the unfor-

*gettable experience of the Weeping Madonnas, which hap-
pened close to our home. I shall gladly make a print of the
picture I had taken of the charred framed picture (not too
sharp), and send it to you in the next couple of days. I am
thankful to God, because we had guardian Angels on the
night of July 19, 1960.*

*There was a frightening electrical storm that night.
Frightening, because a lightning struck the transformer
outside the Restaurant, and also an electrical outlet in my
12 year old daughter's bedroom causing huge flames to
emerge from the electrical outlet. Thank God that no one
was injured.*

*The next day, July 20th, I took my daughter to St.
Paul's to venerate the Icon of the Holy Mother, and to offer
prayers of gratitude. Returning to our gutted Restaurant
and apartment, all that we could see were the charred
ruins. We had lost all our belongings, our clothes and the
Icons we had in our little "Family Altar." My daughter
wept openly for the paper Icon, which I had framed of the
Weeping Madonna. and which she kept near her bed.*

*She had become very attached to it. It truly was
miraculous as to how, with that totally devastating fire this
paper Icon was not burned, as were all our other belongings. Nothing was saved. My daughter kept walking and
searching through the black debris, hoping that the Icon
would be found. Her intuition didn't betray her. All of a
sudden, she looked down and saw the charred Icon, but the
face of the Holy Mother and Christ Child was not burned.
"I found it, I found it" she exclaimed jumping with joy! Our
total disaster was momentarily forgotten, because of our
"treasure" having been found.*

*I took the charred picture and had it framed
between two pieces of glass, and gave it to you to be kept at*

St. Paul's. We'll always consider it a miracle, that our Family was saved from this disastrous fire.

I subsequently moved to Florida for its warm climate, being that I was stricken with multiple sclerosis.

The weather has helped me, and I do not let a day go by without thanking the "Panagia" for the greatest gift to my family.

Respectfully,
Angeliki Pittas

A photo reprint of the original paper Icon. Although hazy, it clearly shows that the devastating fire did not consume the faces of the paper Icon.

Imagine, — a piece of paper being the only item saved from a totally devastating fire! But, — it did happen.

A small part of some bare cement brick walls had been the only thing left standing from the fire; and amid all the charred ruins, the paper copy of the Icon, as you see it in the picture, was the only item salvaged. Indeed a small sign perhaps, — yet a most significant addition to the Mystery of the Icon.

✳   ✳   ✳

Eastern Orthodox Prelates come to reverence the Holy Icons

During the post-Easter season, many Eastern Orthodox Bishops came to venerate the Holy Icons, and hold a Special Service in their own native language.

One of these Prelates was the Most Rev. Metropolitan Boris of Novgorod, Russia. The towering Metropolitan came with a large group of Church Officials and other Dignitaries. With his entourage standing before the Holy Icons, many of who had deep resonant voices, he chanted and prayed in the Slavonic language the identical hymns we chant in Greek in the Greek Orthodox Church. To be

Metropolitan Boris, with Fr. George Papadeas, chants the *"Paraklesis"* Service

sure, this was a great pleasure for all the Orthodox present, who had the opportunity to see and hear the visiting Prelates chant the Orthodox Prayer Service in their native tongue. Their coming from various Orthodox Jurisdictions displayed the universality and unity within the Eastern Orthodox Church Family.

His Excellency Bishop Orestes Chornock of the Carpatho-Russian Greek

Bishop Orestes with Fr. George Papadeas

Orthodox Catholic Church, which is under the jurisdiction of the Greek Orthodox Archdiocese, and the Ecumenical Patriarchate, traveled from his See in Bridgeport to also pray before the Holy Icons. Bishop Orestes was equally amazed, as we all were, to have seen tears emerge from the Icon of the *"Panagia."*

He remarked to the reporter of the **LONG ISLAND PRESS:** *"You feel — but you cannot express your feeling, as you look at this wonderful sight!*

The venerable head of the Russian Orthodox Church outside of the Iron Curtain Metropolitan Anastassy, also came to St. Paul's to pray before the Holy Icons.

He told the Reporters that he came to St. Paul's to pray for all his people, many of whom would not be able to see the Madonna and Her tears.

Metropolitan Anastassy
with Father George Papadeas

When I welcomed him to St. Paul's, he expressed to me a powerful statement of faith when he said: *"I didn't come here to corroborate or investigate, but to venerate."* Truly a profound statement from a great believer! There is no doubt that the Metropolitan must have had many thousands of imitators.

His Eminence Archbishop Palladios of the Ukranian Orthodox Church in the United States, also joined us with his group, and together prayed before the Holy Icons.

Archbishop Palladios
with Fr. Papadeas.

We must not forget that in 1960 the Communists ruled the Soviet Union with an iron hand. The religious persecution was ruthless by the avowed atheistic rulers.

The people of this former glorious Orthodox Territory, where Orthodox Christianity had flourished for centuries, could not openly exercise the only Faith they had ever known, — the Orthodox faith. Who could have ever dreamed that the vast Empire of the Bolsheviks, reigning ruthlessly for over 70 years would crumble in our day, and that the Holy Orthodox Church, like the mythological phoenix, would emerge from the ashes.

The words of St. John the Chrysostom *(Golden-mouthed)*, preached 1600 years ago, amply describe the power and the invincibility of the Church. (Also quoted on page 118).

"When the Church is attacked, She conquers;

When She is scoffed and abused, She emerges even brighter;

She may be tossed about by the waves, but never sinks;

Regardless of how stormy the tempest, it cannot sink the ship of Jesus;

For nothing is more powerful than the Church, which the Lord founded!"

You have just read about some of the Orthodox Dignitaries who came to St. Paul's to venerate the Holy Icons.

As has been noted, while they belong to separate independent Jurisdictions, they are nonetheless Members, and an integral part of the **One, Holy, Catholic and Apostolic Church,** in full communion with each other as they have always been.

The Non-believers

In this great symphony of believers, which has filled many pages of this Book, and which has been sonorous with its melodic harmony of feelings in common, a very weak discord was barely heard from a couple of known non-believers.

They were only one hour away from Hempstead. Yet, they did not take the time to investigate for themselves and then to write accordingly.

Perhaps in their unbelief, they had the fear that they would see a *Phenomenon* which was beyond explanation, and if this had happened, what would their position be, after seeing something that had defied the laws of nature?

Instead, without any attempt to establish or accept the truth for themselves, they chose to publicly reject the *Phenomenon,* which had already been universally espoused.

As human nature goes, I have to assume that they probably have some imitators. But, let us not forget the pro-found teaching of the Parable of the Sower! (p.41).

These non-believers come forth with their own sub-jective conviction, without ever taking the time to investi-gate and to view for themselves. They reject religious *Phenomena* as a general rule, as some even reject that there is a God, the Creator of Heaven and Earth.

Following this line of reasoning, — or better yet, — rejection by preconception, we see a parallel at the time the Lord chastised the Pharisees in Mark 8:18 asking them: *"Are your hearts hardened? Having eyes, do you not see, and having ears, do you not hear?"*

Phenomena, such as the Icons become the object of the non-believers condemning the Church that She *"manufactures"* these, in order to attract people so that they can contribute to the Church.

What can one think or say with this line of frivolous reasoning?

One day I received a letter from Joseph Lewis, President of the **"Free-thinkers of America"** with copies sent simultaneously to all the Editors of the Metropolitan New York Newspapers.

Normally, I would have discarded this letter had it not been for the New York Press. This letter caused a flurry of phone calls from the Editors of the major New York Newspapers. I was asked by them what my response was regarding this letter. My reply was standard, as you shall read presently.

Mr. Lewis condemned the Church for promoting the idea of the *Manifestation,* and stated that he was ready to donate $1,000 (at that time a sizeable amount) to the Red Cross, if I would admit to the *"hoax"* of the tearing Icons, etc.

When I received the barrage of calls from the Editors, my reply was standard. I said: *"Why doesn't Mr. Lewis take the time to make the one hour trip from New York City and see for himself, and if he still wasn't prone to believing, at least he wouldn't have written such baseless accusations.*

How can he doubt all that has been written, not by any Clergyman or Representative of the Church, but by so many Reporters of the esteemed New York Press?

How could he not have been impressed by the inter-views of Scientists and Engineers, all of whom were not of the Orthodox Faith and had no explanation for the 'Phenomenon'?"

I then concluded by saying: *"instead of Mr. Lewis proposing to give $1,000 to the Red Cross if we would deny 'the Hoax,' why doesn't he come to St. Paul's to see and believe for himself this inexplicable in human terms Phenomenon?"*

When this was published, Mr. Lewis was enraged and wrote me another comparable letter, again with copies to the New York Newspapers. He stated something to the effect that my suggestion in reply to his letter would never be, etc.

When I was asked the second time around by the Editors for comments, I responded that I was much too pre-occupied with more important matters, and that I did not have the time to answer such letters. I emphasized, that my reply was given in answer to Mr. Lewis' first letter, and still stood. I never heard from Mr. Lewis again.

Relatively, I was surprised about a year later to read a similar letter of Mr. Lewis, well known for his unfounded attacks on Religious Leaders.

He had sent a caustic letter to Billy Graham, when this famous Preacher had announced that he was going to convene his Crusade in New York City. It was a lengthy let-ter, and among other things Mr. Lewis wrote:

"You know down deep in your heart that the Bible is a fake and a fraud, and has been the most detrimental influ-ence upon the social and intellectual progress of man."

How does one answer such letters? I think the answer is, to not answer.

Not to be outdone by the Freethinkers of America, I received a copy of the satirical Greek language Paper **"The KAMPANA"** (Greek for "bell").

On the front page of the April 30, 1960 edition, there was an article by its Editor, captioned *"THE TEARING PANA-GIAI")* (plural of *"Panagia"*).

In the sub-caption below the title, the Editor presents many sub-titles as follows: **"Distortion of Truth — the 'Panagiai' did not weep. — Paper and wood. — The Archbishop.—Announcements and Pronouncements. — The doves.— At St. Paul's. — Thousands of pilgrims. — The Rev. G. Papadeas. — The human brain. "**

All the above paragraph constitutes the sub-caption to the title of *"THE TEARING PANAGIAI."* I bring to you a true translation of the Article, which commences:

"We are obligated to state the truth. 'The **KAMPANA**' is known that it states the truth in all matters all during the **43** consecutive years it has been publishing. Many friends of 'The **KAMPANA**' ask us if what was written in the Papers, what was announced over the Radio Stations, and what the Television Stations presented are true regarding the Weeping Madonnas, *'great be — their grace'!"*

"We would wish not to write anything absolutely regarding this matter. But we cannot resist, because as we stated above, 'The **KAMPANA**' always tells the truth, and now, not only is the truth distorted but also dignity. "

"Well, now that we are communicating, no Panagia had wept. It was impossible to weep, because the papers and the wood on which the Icons are painted, it is impossible for them to weep, or laugh, regardless of what the interested leaders say, or what many faithful believe that a miracle happened.

They say they saw — that is the Archbishop, the Priest Fr. Papadeas, Reporters and the personnel of the Radio and T.V. Stations, that tears streamed from the eyes of the Panagia."

"The National Herald" (Greek Daily published in Long Island City, N.Y.) in the April 14th 1960 edition reported the *'second miracle'* with full page titles, and in that same edition an announcement of Archbishop Iakovos, who said he saw with his own eyes the Holy Icon weeping and that he would go to the home of Mrs. Koulis, where a special Service would be held before the Icon of the Weeping Virgin."

"And in that same edition a report that yesterday afternoon the Representative of Greece to the United Nations, Mr. Basil Vitsaxis, the Consul of Greece, Mr. Const. Miliaresis, and the Publisher of the National Herald, Mr. Marketos, visited the home of the pious compatriots Mr. and Mrs. P. Koulis, and there offered their respects before the Holy Icon of the Weeping Virgin.

Those three honorable Gentlemen did not say they saw the Icon weep. They only kissed it in veneration."

"The first Icon of the *"Panagia"* began weeping in Long Island in the home of Mr. & Mrs. Peter Catsounis in Island Park. The Archbishop rushed there to hold a blessing Service and the Icon was transported, escorted......by doves to the Church of St. Paul in Hempstead, where it was enshrined on a special Altar, which is being visited by thousands of faithful of every race and national background.

It is said that St. Paul's benefitted from the pilgrims with thousands of dollars, and thus the mortgage of the Church will be paid rapidly. Fr. G. Papadeas, the Pastor, is to be congratulated!... He played his role very well!

The *'miracles'* happened in the midst of New York and in the year **1960,** when only the human brain, which God gave him makes miracles!"

Thus ended the unbelievable article published in *"The KAMPANA"*

(Author's Note: I included this article of The KAMPANA, even though it is a Paper with limited readership, to show how blinded people choose to become, and how they shy away from that which is certified by so many people! The Editor stated that for 43 years he has always published the *"truth,"* and that he was being asked by many of his readers if what was written in the N.Y. Newspapers and shown over TV is true. You read what he answered! Truly unbelievable!)

Seeing an article like the above, which I translated from the Greek, truly makes one wonder! How could such irresponsible and false statements be printed? How could people subscribe to such a Newspaper? One person, through his own satyrical Paper defies the testimony of eminent Clergymen, Batteries of Reporters of the N.Y. Press, Scientists, Engineers, etc.!

Without a personal visit to St. Paul's even out of curiosity to view for himself and form his opinion, the Editor without any idea of what was happening at St. Paul's chose to write subjectively in his satirical style. Is this objective reporting expected of a Newspaper?

Was it beneath him to accept that, which was seen by old and young alike? By those of limited education, and those with high academic degrees? By the working man and by the professional? By the battery of Reporters, who without exception were totally astounded with these *Phenomena?*

I wonder what runs through some people's minds, and how they perceive realities. For me, there can only be one answer, and that is, the fear that they wouldn't be able to cope with a reality, because of their preconceptions. They would probably fear of how could they ever give an explanation, when with their own eyes they would be seeing some supernatural, inexplicable phenomenon!

The Editor of **"The KAMPANA"** gleaned the news articles of the major New York Newspapers, and then, according to what he was predisposed to believe, he printed his own version in his Newspaper.

He started his article by stating that *"his Paper has always brought forth the truth to the people for a history of 43years!"* I must presume that some people have their own definition of *"truth!"*

I really wasn't going to include the above article in this Book, but his ideas possibly may represent the opinions even of a few others, who stand from afar and make judgements and pronouncements, according to the way they feel, or, of what may be beneficial to them. I do not recall, which of the ancient sages stated: **"You cannot convince me, even though you may convince me!"** How true!

People who think like the Editor of this satirical Paper seem to have one opinion in common; that the Church is just a place to collect money.

The Publisher of **"The KAMPANA"** talks about the Church collecting thousands of dollars, which would rapidly pay off the Mortgage!

How would he know? Where did he get his information? He must have estimated by some fast personal multiplication tables. These proceeds couldn't even commence to pay the alleged Mortgage.

At any rate, it appears that the Publisher of **The KAMPANA** and Mr. Lewis must have earned their **"Degree"** from the same school!

The fact remains, that these *"Divine Signs"* were accepted and certified by the most responsible and reputable sources. Hundreds of thousands, went through St. Paul's to view the Icons. Eminent Prelates and Professors of the scientific world rendered their comments, and the Reporters of the New York Newspapers reported as they saw the *"Signs."*

It was very moving to witness the piety with which the thousands approached to revere the Icons. The reverence they displayed and the emotion reflected on their faces was continually witnessed before the Holy Icons at the St. Paul's Cathedral.

The spiritual aura, was a constant refreshing factor. I feel confident, that the persons who made the Pilgrimage to St. Paul's were spiritually enriched. Standing there before the Icons in prayer or meditation, I think that even for a moment they were transported into the spiritual realm!

The *"Portaitissa"* Icon
"All-Holy Mother of the Portals, or Gate" at the Iveron Monastery

To have a clearer understanding of the second Weeping Madonna, I think it is important to bring to you some historical facts regarding the Monastery of Iveron, which was blessed ten centuries ago with the Holy Icon, known as the *"Portaitissa,"* *"All-Holy Mother"* of Iveron.

Since the time this Icon was found by the Monks of the Iveron Monastery in 1054 A.D., it has been enshrined there.

The title of the Monastery in Greek is pronounced **"Iveron."** * **(Ee-VEE-rone).** Actually it should be "Iberon," because the first monks of the Monastery hailed from "Iberia," which today is the Nation of Georgia, bordering Russia.

The Monastery of Iveron on Mount Athos was established in 980 A.D. by the Iberian General John Tornikios and his two nephews George and Efthimios, who became the first Monks of the Monastery. Subsequently, other Monks followed from Iberia.

The language spoken in all the 20 massive Monasteries of Mount Athos was Greek, except in the Monastery of Iveron, where the language was Iberian.

However, by 1355 A.D., Greek, the overpowering and dominant language of culture, and of the Holy Scriptures, supplanted the Iberian language. Now in all the 20 Monasteries the spoken language is Greek.

The citizens of Georgia, whose ancestors were known as Iberians have always been predominantly Orthodox Christian. In fact, Georgia is one of the first Christian Nations, dating back to the first centuries of Christianity.

Another fact of recent history is, that the President of Georgia Edouard Schevernadze had been the Foreign Minister of the Soviet Union under Michael Gorbachev.

Being an Official of the Soviet Union then, an atheistic regime, it was taken for granted, as with all the Leaders of the Soviet Union, that he too was an atheist, — at least on the surface. Proof of this statement is, that he was baptized an Orthodox Christian soon after he became the Country's President.

When the Soviet Union was dismantled in 1990, Georgia, like other peripheral Countries bordering Russia, regained her independence. Most of these former Nations of the Soviet Union, like Georgia are almost 100% Orthodox Christian.

The Churches of these Orthodox Countries, after many decades of persecutions, emerged from the underground to re-establish themselves in their respective Orthodox Countries.

For 70 years the ruthless Dictators of the Soviet Union went to every extreme to annihilate the Christian Orthodox Religion from their totalitarian State.

----

* (In Greek the letter **"b"** in Iberia is softened, sounding like the letter **"v."** Hence, in Greek we say **"Iveron"** instead of **Iberon**. There is no letter **"b"** in the Greek alphabet. Euphonically, I think "Iveron" sounds softer than "Iberon." I chose to use **"Iveron"** in English).

It is estimated that under Stalin's rule alone, over 20,000,000 Orthodox Christians were killed; among them thousands of Bishops and Priests. It was no different under all the successive atheistic regimes during the seven decades of oppression, when preaching or practicing Christianity was strictly prohibited.

The Dictators of the Soviet Union, as well as other persecutors of the Church in all ages had forgotten, or were fanatically blinded to the degree that they could not discern the truth.

Indeed, these atheists were totally foreign to the verse of St. John the Evangelist, who eloquently stated in his First Epistle, Chapter 5, verse 4:

"For whatever is born of God, overcomes the world; and this is the victory, that has overcome the world — our faith!":

St. John the Chrysostom (Greek for 'Golden-mouthed'), Patriarch of Constantinople, lived in the 4th Century A.D. He bequeathed to all the Orthodox Churches the Divine Liturgy, universally celebrated until today throughout the world, wherever there is an Orthodox Church. He was a prolific writer, having given us so many volumes with commentaries on the Epistles of St. Paul.

In one of his sermons, (as already quoted on page 108), describing the invincibility of the Church, among other things, this Church luminary stated:

"When the Church is attacked, She conquers;

When She is scoffed and abused, She emerges even brighter;

She may be tossed about by the waves, but never sinks;

Regardless of how stormy the tempest, it cannot sink the ship of Jesus;

For nothing is more powerful than the Church, which the Lord founded!"

Indisputable proof of the above paragraph is the fact, that the Soviet Communistic totalitarian reign of over 70 years totally collapsed. **The Dictatorship crumbled, but the Church once again emerged triumphantly.**

Some Facts regarding the Original *"Portaitissa"* Icon

It is interesting to learn some of the facts regarding the origin of the Holy Icon of the *"Portaitissa."*

Late in the 8th Century, A.D. there arose in the Byzantine Empire the tumultuous and very perilous period of Iconoclasm.

("Iconoclasm," is a composite Greek term meaning the breaking, or destroying of Icons).

The Iconoclasts brought great strife to Eastern Christendom lasting for about 100 years. These extremists, with unbelievable fanaticism, set out to destroy every Icon that they could find.

It wasn't until the 7th Ecumenical Council in 787 A.D., that the Council came forth to clarify the relevance of Icons to the faith of the Christians.

The declaration was, that the Saints depicted on the Icons were only to be venerated and not worshipped. Worship belongs only to God. The faithful simply give homage to the Saint or Saints portrayed on the Icons.

During this destructive period of Iconoclasm, blind fanaticism was the norm. We can understand this to a certain degree, when even today, people blinded by fanaticism set out to destroy that, which in their judgement think should not exist?

Down through the ages so many have suffered even death, having become victims of blind fanatics.

Such was the case of the Iconoclasts, whose life's mission was to destroy every Icon they could find and possibly torture their owners. Unfortunately, what helped them in their fanatic drive was, that they had the political backing of that time.

In Nicaea, a city on the shores of Asia Minor, near Constantinople, there lived a pious widowed mother with her son. Their prize possession was a masterfully painted Icon of the *All-Holy Mother holding the Christ Child in Her arms.*

It is not unrealistic that there are some Icons, which excel in transmitting the feeling of an in depth religious experience. The original Icon of the *"Portaitissa"* is one of these. It was, as stated, the precious possession of this widowed mother and her son.

Having heard that the Iconoclasts in making their rounds would soon be coming to her house to destroy the Icon, and even punish her and her son for keeping the Icon, she decided to cast the Icon into the Aegean Sea with a prayer of hope, that one day it would fall into the hands of a true believer.

Early one morning she walked to the seashore with her son and after offering her prayer she cast the Icon into the Sea.

It was a very painful decision, but they both were comforted that the Icon would escape the fanaticism of the Iconoclasts.

To their astonishment, their Icon showed forth its first sign of *miraculous* expression by not falling flatly into the sea as would have been natural, to float along over the waves. Instead, the Icon stood upright, riding over the waves, as the astounded mother and son kept watching until it disappeared on the horizon.

The Mother said to her son: *"Never forget this my child. You have witnessed one of God's many wonders!"*

The mother was greatly comforted after having witnessed such a manifestation. This fortified her belief that the precious Icon, which manifested itself in such a miraculous manner, would surely fall into the proper hands.

Having cast her very precious Icon into the sea, she sensed a strong maternal premonition. She became very apprehensive having heard rumors that she might be betrayed to the Iconoclasts. Her concern was not what would happen to her. She agonized for the fate of her son. The only solution for his safety was, for him to be taken far away from Nicaea. Quickly, she made all the necessary arrangements, and her son was soon en route to Salonika (Thessaloniki), Greece.

Soon after the son arrived in Salonika, he would make his first visit to the nearest Church and introduce himself to the Priest. He would offer his help in any Church project during his every free hour. Thus, it wasn't long before his association with the Clergy and visiting Monks from nearby Mount Athos, had begun to have a strong influence on him. His spirit nurtured by his pious mother was being further enriched.

He was truly inspired by the holiness of the monastic life. Deeply within his soul he felt a calling from God, and made his decision to dedicate his life to the Lord. Finding his way to Mount Athos, and submitting to the austere regimentation of the monastic life he was tonsured a Monk.

At the Iveron Monastery the young Monk was surrounded with many beautiful Icons, but his love for the Icon, which he helped toss into the sea from the shores of Asia Minor a few years ago had never waned.

In this deeply religious atmosphere, where Icons were in view everywhere, he would relate on occasion to his brother Monks, and also to the visitors coming to the Monastery of Iveron, the story of his precious Icon, and how it showed its first miraculous sign by standing upright in the wavy sea.

Before long, this storied Icon had become a legend, with a rippling effect on the whole peninsula of Mount Athos.

The widow's son already had spent many years as a devoted and dedicated Monk at the Monastery. Ripe in years, he finally passed on from this world to meet the Lord, Whom he so deeply worshipped.

During his time, the Monastery was a very small one. But a few years after his passing, a huge Monastery was erected, retaining the title "Monastery of Iveron." For over a century, the story of the Icon had been repeated numerous times, until the year 1004 A.D.

One evening, before the regularly scheduled Vespers, the Monks were relaxing on the Monastery grounds over-looking the sea. From afar they saw an unusual sight.

It resembled a pillar of fire reaching from the sea upwardly toward the sky. The object kept approaching toward the shore of the Monastery where the Monks were gathered.

Steadily, coming toward their direction in a vertical position, they recognized the Icon, about which they had heard so many times.

Reverently taking the Icon in their hands, they offered prayers of gratitude and chanted the two word prayer over and over again: "*KEE-ree-eh Eh-LEH-ee-sone*" (Lord, have mercy). In a religious procession they climbed the hill to the Monastery and enshrined the Icon in the "*Katholikon,*" (Greek term for the main Church of a Monastery).

The Monks kept a vigil praying for most of the night having before them the Object of their devotion.

It can be noted here, that there is a special affection and devotion to the *"All Holy Mother"* by all the Monks of the Mount Athos Monasteries. This can easily be understood, because all the 20 Monasteries collectively are known as ***"The Garden of the Panagia!"***

The Iveron Monastery as it appears today. It is there that the original *"Portaitissa"* Holy Icon is enshrined.

The Monks of Iveron now had the precious Icon of the *Holy Mother,* which by virtue of the way it arrived at the Monastery was in itself a *"miraculous"* happening. During this Vigil, I would venture to say that some Monks would have brought to mind the all-night vigil held in the Church of Vlachernae in Constantinople, after the Queen City was saved from the siege of the barbaric Avars in 626 A.D.

I say this, because in all the Monasteries, the ageless and most inspiring Service of *"The Akathist Hymn"* is often prayed.

It was very late that night, when the Monks of the Iveron Monastery retired to sleep for a little while, and then rise after a few hours for the daily early dawn Devotional Prayers.

Having entered the Church at daybreak, they noticed that the Icon, which only hours before had been enshrined on a little *"Altar"* was missing. Making a thorough search, they were unable to find it until later, when one of the Monks saw the Icon hanging under the central arch of the Monastery gate.

How could the Icon have gotten there in the few hours they had been apart from it? Who put it there, and for what purpose? Truly mysterious! The Icon was removed from the arch, and placed once again on the same little *"Altar,"* as had been done the previous night. The next morning the scene was repeated.

This time the Monks rushed to the gate and behold, the Icon once again was hanging from the arch above the gate.

It was then decided by the Monks that the *"All-Holy Mother"* must have wanted to have Her Icon hung over the gate to guard, as it were, the portals of the Monastery.

Eventually a Chapel was erected over the gate area, where the Holy Icon is still enshrined today. Hence the term *"Portaitissa." ("Mother of the Portals.")*

On the lithographed print of the *"Portaitissa"* Icon we see a wound painted, with blood dripping from the cheek of the *Holy Mother.* This was another sign of Her *"miraculous"* expression, as we shall presently see.

Not long after the Icon was enshrined by the Monks at the Iveron Monastery, some pirates disembarked on the Holy Mountain to loot the Monasteries.

One of those pirates, a Moslem, seeing the Holy Icon over the gate, sadistically sought to deface the Icon by piercing the *Panagia's* cheek with his bayonet. Immediately from the cheek of that painted Image, blood commenced to flow as from a live person. Totally overcome by shock and fear, seeing what he could not possibly have imagined or understood, the Pirate reasoned that some *"Higher Power"* was being revealed to him.

He fell to his knees trembling with great fear, and with hands raised he prayed in the best way he knew how to some *"Supreme Being."*

His horrible act would ultimately result in his conversion. He would never be the same man again. His spiritually blinded eyes had finally been opened, so that now he could clearly discern the serenity reflected on the Monks' faces, as compared to his life; — a life of misery, anxiety, intrigue, looting, pillaging and murdering. For the first time he felt a serenity he had never known, and deeply within his soul for the first time in his life he sensed a fulfilling peace. It was as if he had suddenly discovered Paradise on earth.

Brimming over with inexpressible spiritual joy, he deeply felt a true rebirth, and then made the decision to become a part of this serene atmosphere, providing the Monks would accept him. Remorseful for his past ghastly deeds, and with soul-cleansing repentance he asked the Brotherhood to find it in their hearts to forgive him.

He placed himself at their mercy, and was willing to submit to any duty that would be assigned to him, in order that he could have the great privilege of becoming part of that heavenly environment.

It wasn't long, after having fully repented for all his past sinful life, which included his last evil act of desecrating the Icon of the *Holy Mother,* that he received instruction in the Christian Faith and was baptized. This former enemy of the Church, had now become a brother to his former *"infidel"* enemies; he was tonsured a Monk, and dedicated his life in the service of God, until he was summoned by the Lord. His spiritual rebirth in Christ was a true miracle,

The Russian Connection

Since then, many miracles have been attributed to the *"Portaitissa"* Icon. Perhaps the most noted of these, because of the personality involved, was the miraculous healing of the Russian Czar Alexis' daughter in the year 1648 A.D.

The Czar, having heard of the miraculous cures wrought by the Holy Mother's Icon of Iveron, sent a delegation to firstly request permission from the *Ecumenical Patriarch* in Constantinople, and then from the *"Hegoumenos"* (Abbot) of the Iveron Monastery.

His request was for the Holy Icon to be brought to the Royal Family for veneration. He believed, that in prayer before the Icon, the *"All-Holy Mother"* would intercede to Her Son for the cure of his daughter of her serious illness.

The devoted Monks of the Monastery were apprehensive. They feared that if the Icon was taken to Russia it probably would never be returned. The Monks of Iveron lost no time.

Through one of their talented Brothers an exact replica was painted and given to the Czar's delegation. The Czar happily received the Icon, even if it was a replica.

The Royal Family prayed fervently before the Icon of the *"All-Holy Mother and Child"* in the Chapel of the Palace. Their faith was profound and all encompassing. The *miracle* did happen, and the Czar's daughter was healed.

At this point, I would like to stress that contrary to what some people may believe, it is not the Icon, or any religious article of itself, which brings forth a miracle. These are but means. It is the prayer in faith of individuals or groups, whatever the case may be, that brings forth miracles.

St. James in his Epistle in the New Testament, chapter 5, verses 14-15, states:

"Is anyone sick among you? Let him call the Presbyters (Priests) of the Church; and let them pray over him, anointing him with oil in the Name of the Lord; and the prayer of faith shall save the sick."

Here we notice, that from the first years of the formally organized Christian Church, She is present to minister to the spiritually needs of Her people. In the above verse we readily see:

1) The Presbyters were ordained by the Apostles.
2) These Presbyters belonged to a specific Church — the One, Holy, Catholic and Apostolic Church.
3) The prayer of faith is a prerequisite for healing.
4) The *"anointing with oil"* (an external sign of therapeutic value) is the Sacrament of Holy Unction as practiced in the Orthodox Churches from the Apostolic times.

The healing of the Czar's daughter firmly established the *"Portaitissa"* Icon of Iveron, as the special Protectress of the Russian people.

Since that period, and until 1932, the Iveron Monastery was the recipient of many gifts and subsidies from the faithful of Russia.

To be sure, in our days here in America, we may not have had with us the original Icon of Iveron, but only an inexpensive lithographed copy of the *"Portaitissa"* on Long Island. But, — even through this very simple medium, God in His Omniscience and Omnipotence designated the *"Sign"* of the tearing Icons to primarily work *"miracles"* in the hearts of His people in our troubled times.

Traditions bring Fulfillment

As I have written in this Book, there have been comparable *Manifestations* in Greece, prior to the ones witnessed in Long Island. Shrines have been instituted in various parts of Greece, which are a source of spiritual nourishment for so many pilgrims.

I would presume, that comparable *"Signs"* from *Above* may have been experienced in other Countries.

After all, does not the Psalmist David state in Psalm 24, verse 1,

"The earth is the Lord's, and the fulness thereof; the world, and those who dwell in it?"

My purpose in writing this Book was not to research *"Divine Signs"* witnessed throughout the world. This would be a voluminous project. I simply have concentrated on what has been my personal experience, and to record it, as the Events unfolded and witnessed by so many.

The *"Divine Signs"* of the three Holy Icons was very important religiously and historically, and I felt compelled by conscience to record the facts as they happened, and to share them with as many people as possible,— even after 40 years!

If this Book had not been written, perhaps the *Supernatural Manifestations of the "Divine Signs"* may have become to a great or lesser degree forgotten. I never would want this to happen.

Therefore, I recorded all the facts as they evolved, so as to become a living and perpetual history.

These facts are authentic in every respect, because I have lived them intimately, as have so many others.

I further believe, that this Book will bring back many beautiful and uplifting memories, and that it will rekindle the hearts of the hundreds of thousands, who passed through St. Paul's, as well as to those, who repeatedly read about the *Manifestations* in the excellent Press coverage, or viewed them on Television.

It also will relate to so many others, who were too young during the year of the Manifestations to know that God speaks to the world with *"Signs"* at various times.

But, in order to commence understanding these *"Signs,"* it is vital that the spiritual eyes of our hearts are open at all times.

As stated, there are many Shrines in Greece. The ones that I have visited, or read about, were founded as a result of a *"Sign from Above."* However, there is one difference, as compared to the *"Signs"* witnessed within the area of St. Paul's Parish. There is no case documented of three successive Weeping Icons of our *"All-Holy Mother, the Ever-Virgin Mary,"* — or even of any other three consecutive *"Signs"* or *"Manifestations"* in any one area.

I feel that God chose America, and specifically our beloved St. Paul's Family in Long Island, to invite the world in a very special way to a spiritual Banquet!

Mr. & Mrs. Peter Catsounis had given St. Paul's their Weeping Madonna, which was an Icon of the Western Iconographic tradition.

Subsequently, Mr. & Mrs. Peter Koulis gave their Icon of the *"Portaitissa"* of the Byzantine tradition to St. Paul's for the thousands to have an opportunity to venerate.

So many thoughts went through my mind thinking of these Holy Icons. One such thought was the fact that the Icons had come from two different Iconographic traditions, that is, one from the Western or Papal Church, and the other two from the Byzantine tradition.

Then to think, that the third Weeping Icon, in every respect a masterful Icon of the traditional Byzantine Iconography is now in Rome since the 15th Century.

These Icons bring to mind the unfortunate Schism of 1054 A.D., when the cleavage came between the Western, or Papal Church, and the Eastern Orthodox Church.

Although separated from each other for almost 946 years, they are often referred to as Sister Churches, having a valid Priesthood and the Seven Sacraments, through which we receive the Divine and Saving Grace of our Lord.

As noted previously, the prayer for re-union is always heard in all the Orthodox Liturgies. It is hoped that the on-going Catholic-Orthodox dialogues and consultations will gain momentum to effect this unity and help to heal the 946 years of separation.

Now, living in our modern 21st Century, with its unbelievable technological advances, and so many and varied changes constantly being experienced, the Holy Orthodox Church still stands today very firm and strong, adhering to the ageless beliefs and traditions of the undivided Church.

After all, does not the Apostle to the Nations St. Paul admonish us in 2 Thessalonians 2:15?

"Therefore Brethren, stand fast, and hold the traditions which you have been taught, whether by word, or our epistle."

I think that one of the shortcomings of our life today in America today is, that we are sorely lacking in traditions in many ways.

Traditions enrich life. They are the spice of life. They give us substance and meaning to life. They give us a sense of fulfillment. In the Orthodox realm one can attest to this, by the many Church traditions and Rituals celebrated today in the Orthodox Churches, as they were from the Apostolic times.

Traditions, such as the 40 day blessing of every newborn, as mentioned in the Preface, as also the traditional Service of Blessing the five loaves, — an offering of love made by Parishioners, after which all the Congregation receives a slice of the sweetened bread, figuratively partaking as the one family of God in common at the same table.

This brief Service is symbolic of the Lord's feeding the five thousand in the wilderness, after He had preached to them. (Matthew 14:13-21).

These, and so many other traditions which bring the Bible to life are very much alive, and practiced mostly in the Eastern Orthodox Church.

Iconography is no exception. Without question, Byzantine Iconography can easily be understood as a powerful, soul-stirring, fulfilling, and most certainly a very strong tradition.

The Eastern Orthodox Churches, richly adorned with Icons, serve to put the worshipper in a religious frame of mind. Surrounded by the numerous colorful Icons and murals adorning huge wall spaces, the worshipper cannot help but bring to mind, who and what they represent. The Holy Icons are a teaching in themselves — a type of visual catechism, or instruction.

Icons are also a vital part of every Orthodox home, for prayers and veneration. The Icon is nothing less than an added, helpful medium for our contact with the Divine!

Over the past decades I have purchased many volumes on Byzantine Iconography, and have collected many prints of masterpieces from the prolific era of Byzantine Iconography.

One of my favorite Icons is *"The Hodegetria" Icon. (One who directs, or shows the way).* This Icon is titled in the Roman Catholic Church as *"The Mother of Perpetual Help."* The prototype of this Icon is traditionally believed to have been painted by St. Luke the Evangelist.

Through this prototype, which has consistently been the inspirational model for the Byzantine Iconographers down through the ages, the Church has been enriched with great masterpieces.

Some years ago I had purchased two lithographed copies of this beautiful Icon of *"The Hodegetria"* and had them appropriately framed. One for my home and the other for my office.

When the Koulis family had donated their Weeping Madonna to St. Paul's, I thought it would be a very good gesture to present to them one of these Icons to fill the empty space left on their *"Family Altar."* It also was an Icon of the *"Panagia with the Christ Child"* as was the *"Portaitissa,"* which they had donated to St. Paul's, but by a different Iconographer. I knew they would be very pleased.

In retrospect, I seemed to have been roaming in a realm of wonderful happenings and coincidences. The spiritual aura was ever-present, affording me a steady buoyant feeling. Never did a day go by, that I didn't have the pleasure of meeting some Dignitary of our Church, as well as many Clergymen from the various Denominations.

Precisely during that time, when I was making final plans to present this Icon to the Koulis Family, I received a call from a distinguished Prelate and esteemed Friend, the Bishop of New England, His Grace Athenagoras Kokkinakis.

I treasured his friendship for over 25 years. What a blessed coincidence, I thought to myself, for him to have called me. He told me that he was pleased to have read the various articles in the Boston Newspapers about the Icons of the Weeping Madonna, and that he planned to come to St. Paul's to venerate the Icons, and officiate at the Divine Liturgy the first weekend after Easter.

I was elated that this much loved Prelate would visit St. Paul's, and thought that this was a wonderful opportunity to have him make the presentation of the Icon to the Koulis Family, which for them would have added significance.

When Bishop Athenagoras arrived from Boston, he requested that I take him to St. Paul's to pray the *"Paraklesis"* Service before checking into the Garden City Hotel. Approaching the Church, the Bishop was amazed to see the long line of people waiting to enter the Church.

We entered through the Sacristy for the Bishop to wear his vestments. Before commencing the Service he asked the visitors, who had filled the Church to join him in prayer in the Devotional Service of the *"Paraklesis,"* in honor of the Holy Mother.

After the Service he spoke eloquently about the relevance of the Ever-Virgin Mary in the life of the Orthodox Christians through the Ages. I watched the people in the pews, and was happy to see how attentive they all were, especially since for the most part they were people from other Faiths. Subsequently he blessed all present, much to their pleasure.

Meeting in my office after the Service, among other things we discussed was the procedure for the following day's Divine Liturgy. I had asked that after the Liturgy the Bishop would present the Icon of *"The Hodegetria"* to Mr. and Mrs. Peter Koulis in behalf of, and with the blessings of His Eminence Archbishop Iakovos.

It was an inspiring Divine Liturgy, during which His Grace, having lived and studied in Constantinople for many years, celebrated the Divine Liturgy with all the magnificence of Byzantine grandeur! After the Liturgy, with his well known eloquence, he addressed the Koulis Family in loving terms before the capacity Congregation. His Grace then presented to them the Icon of *"The Hodegetria,"* or *"Mother of Perpetual Help"* in behalf of the Archbishop, congratulating and thanking them for having donated their Weeping Icon to St. Paul's. The Koulis family was visibly moved, and accepted the gift with much gratitude.

It was generally felt that Bishop Athenagoras' Pastoral visit was another milestone for St. Paul's, especially coinciding at a time when everyone was psychologically tuned in with the prevailing spirit, as a result of the *"Divine Signs."*

Mrs. Koulis surprised, and awed by the Third Weeping Madonna

"Panagia the Hodegetria" "Mother of Perpetual Help"

About two weeks after Bishop Athenagoras' visit, that is, Saturday, May 7, 1960, Mrs. Antonia Koulis excitedly called to tell me that the Icon which we had presented to her was tearing profusely; even more than the Icon which she had donated to St. Paul's less than a month before.

When I heard this totally unexpected news, I cannot begin to describe what I personally felt at that moment!

My first thought was, how could this be happening again and in the same house in such a brief span of time? What does it all mean? What would people start thinking?

I treasured my personal experience with the Icons, and the verification by all of the first two Icons. Without question — not even for a moment did I ever doubt that a third *"Sign"* had come in our midst through another Weeping Icon. I thought to myself, *"after all, is not the number three the holiest of all numbers for us?"*

But, how can anyone not believe, when it comes to God's will and expression? — When through *"Divine Signs"* the laws of nature are challenged and overcome? — When the simplicity, with which God chooses to bring *Manifestations* before us, is undeniably wiser, and more powerful than anything human? This is what I believe.

I thank God that Mrs. Koulis called me first. Over the phone I pleaded with her not to breathe a word to anyone. I didn't want the people congregating once again around her home, as had happened with the *"Portaitissa"* Icon.

I thought that the Icon had to be moved and immediately to St. Paul's, where a Shrine had already been established.

I told her I would be arriving at her home presently to take the Icon and place it next to the other two.

She readily consented. I sensed the feeling that she didn't want to be taxed all over again, as she was about a month ago along with her whole family, by having to contend with the few thousand, who had passed through her apartment to view the second Holy Icon.

When I arrived, Mrs. Koulis was waiting at the door and we both proceeded directly to the *"Family Altar"* to see the third Weeping Icon. I literally froze. It was a sight to behold! Even more powerful than the Holy Icon of Iveron!

The tears were forming in rapid succession at the eyes, then falling into the wet tracks already formed down the "All-*Holy Mother's"* cheeks, onto Her garment, to reach the bottom of the frame.

It was for me a highly spiritually charged emotional moment. I found myself totally focused and absorbed with this newest *"Phenomenon from Above."* Once again, God was speaking much louder to us all!

I strongly felt the need to pray the spiritually uplifting *"Paraklesis"* Service before the Icon; to beseech our Lord to bless us, to mellow our hearts, to humble us, to strengthen us, and to spiritually enlighten us to gain a clearer understanding of His word; to give us some message through the *Holy Mother's* tears on the three Icons!

After the *"Paraklesis"* Service, although I had no questions or doubts, I took it upon myself to open the back of the Icon, just to verify if it was dry as was the *"Portaitissa"* Icon. It was no surprise to see that it was just as dry.

Holding the glassed frame after removing the Icon print, I gazed at the glass with amazement and awe.

On the glass, there were two definite streams of tears; one commencing from a slightly higher point than the other.

It was the perfect match for the position of the tears on the Icon print, being that the *"All-Holy Mother's"* head pictured on the Icon is slightly tilted.

Upon returning to St. Paul's, I immediately placed this Icon next to the other two. Now, there were three Holy Icons, and I couldn't help but associate them with the holiness of the number *"three!"*

The Origin of the Third Icon
"Panagia the Hodegetria" *"Mother of Perpetual Help"*

At this point I would like to acquaint you in the next few paragraphs, not only with the history of this Icon, but the significance of the portrayals painted by the talented and inspired Iconographer of this masterpiece.

On the Icon on page 141 you can clearly see the definition and the symbols of *"The Hodegetria"* Icon.

Having placed the *"Panagia Hodegetria"* next to the Icons
of the *"Mother of Sorrows"* and the *"Portaitissa,"* Fr. Papadeas prayed
the *"Paraklesis"* Service.

The Holy Icon of *"Panagia the Hodegetria"* gives credence to the fact, that the masters of Iconography prayed and fasted before applying their first stroke on the piece of wood before them. There can be no other explanation for the uniqueness of so many Icons from the Byzantine Era.

These Icons have been classified in a separate, distinctive and hallowed category.

"Icon," the Greek word for *"Image,"* is a visual object. When we view an Icon, we can instantly be drawn closer to the reality of God, as well as the many Saints, our Brothers and Sisters in Heaven, interceding in our behalf.

As explained, the Orthodox Churches are adorned with many Icons, commencing with the *"Pantocrator,"* the *"Panagia,"* the Prophets of the Old Testament, the Holy Apostles, the Great Church Fathers, the Saints of the undivided Christian Church, as well as many Biblical scenes, mainly from the life and Passion of our Lord, crowned with the Glorious Resurrection. In this manner, the theology of the Bible is vividly brought to life through Byzantine Iconography in the Orthodox Churches.

There was of course the traditional prototype Icon of the *"Panagia,"* reputedly the work of St. Luke, who was not only a physician, but traditionally believed to have painted the first Icon of the Virgin Mary holding the Christ Child. St. Luke's Icon was given the name of *"Panagia Hodegetria,"* (*the "All-Holy," who leads, or shows the way*). This Icon became the prototype for subsequent Iconographers, who bequeathed us with masterpieces.

As noted, the Icon of *"The Hodegetria"* or *"Mother of Perpetual Help,"* was the work of an inspired and devoted Iconographer of the Cretan School, probably painted about the 15th Century.

This particular Icon of the 15th century Artist from the Island of Crete was stolen from a Church by a wine merchant and taken to Rome for reasons that only he knew.

The speculation is, that perhaps he wanted to rescue the Icon from the invading Mohammedan Turks, or to be reimbursed in some fashion for his efforts. But his plan never materialized, because he was stricken with a terminal illness.

Sensing that his end was near, he gave the Icon to a friend with the request that he give it to a Church. On March 27, 1499 the Holy Icon was taken to the Church of St. Matthew, where it inspired the thousands of pilgrims for 300 years. When Napoleon entered Rome in 1798 along with other buildings the St. Matthew Church was leveled to the ground. The Holy Icon was secretly taken by an Augustinian Monk to be discovered 67 years later.

By an edict of Pope Pius IX the Holy Icon was placed in the Church of St. Alphonsus, constructed over the leveled Church of St. Matthew.

Many thousands converge annually to view and be blessed by the Icon of the *"Mother of Perpetual Help"* hanging today over the Altar of the St. Alphonsus Church.

The masterful Cretan Iconographer had portrayed the *All-Holy Mother* holding the Christ Child on Her left arm.

At the top of the Icon on either side of the Ever-Virgin's halo we see the Greek letters **"MP"** and **"ΘY"** with a slur on top connecting each set of two letters. We notice such contractions on many Byzantine Icons. (See Holy Icon for inscriptions p.141).

In the Byzantine Iconographic era it became standard for the Iconographers to use contractions. These consisted of the first and last letter of each adjective, noun or name.

The first and last letters of a name had a slur over them to denote that the omitted letters in the middle were understood.

For example **"MP"** means **"Mother,"** (the English letter **"P"** is the **"R"** in the Greek alphabet). **"ΘY"** means **"of God."**

Looking at *"The Hodegetria,"* or *"Mother of Perpetual Help"* Icon, below the contractions for *"Mother of God,"* we see the contractions for the Archangel Michael to the left, and that of Archangel Gabriel to the right.

The Archangel Michael is holding the instruments of the Lord's Passion, that is, the lance and the reed with the sponge dipped in vinegar and gall sadistically given to our suffering Lord to drink, when in the midday scorching sun He exclaimed in agony: *"I thirst!"*

The Archangel Gabriel is holding the Cross and the nails used to fasten the hands and the feet of our Lord to the Cross.

We notice also, that the Holy Mother's mouth is rather small, denoting silent recollection. Her eyes are directed toward us, and are rather large, to encompass or look out as it were, for all of us, Her children.

The Christ Child portrays a feeling of safety, as any child senses being held securely in His Mother's arms! There is a halo around the Christ Child's head with a cross outlined, on which we notice the Greek letters **"O"** on the left side, **"Ω"** (Greek Omega) on top of His Head, and **"N"** on the right side.

These three letters constitute two words in Greek, the article with the noun, **"O ΩN,"** meaning: **"The One Who is!"**

To the right of the halo, we see a double set of letters with the slur on the top. These are the first and letters of Jesus Christ, **"IC" "XC."** (in Greek, **"I**ησου**C X**ριστο**C**).**" The background of the Icon is golden, symbolic of Heaven.

We also notice, that one of the Holy Child's sandals is loosened hanging from the lace. There is a worthy symbolic tale regarding this. The Child Jesus is supposed to have seen the Archangels carrying some of the instruments of His future torture, and in fear hastened to run to His Mother, knowing that He would be secure in Her arms. We can see this by His hands, tightly clutching the hand of His Mother.

In His haste while running to reach His Mother, one of His sandals was loosened, but is still clinging onto His foot by a single string.

This is symbolic of every soul seeking to cling to Christ, even by one last thread.

We also see that the Child Jesus is not looking toward His Mother, but at the Archangel Gabriel, expressing in a manner that now He has no fear, because He is secure in His Mother's arms!

Yes, there is great beauty, as there are meaningful symbolisms in this particular Icon.

We can rightfully then say, that Icons are not only beautiful as works of art. They are prolific in symbolism, in life-giving instruction and of profound theological content. It is no wonder that the Icons have been so appropriately labeled: **"Windows to Heaven.**

St. Paul's Faithful
Venerate Holy Icons after every Liturgy

It was Saturday, May 7,1960, when I brought the third weeping Icon to St, Paul's.

I prayed the *"Paraklesis"* Service, after which I spoke about *"The Hodegetria"* to the Congregation, who had compacted the Church, and via the speakers to the many outside the Church, waiting patiently for their turn to view the two Icons. I surprised everyone, — and a few light gasps were heard, when I announced the fact about the *Manifestation* of a third Icon.

A lithographed copy of the original Eastern Orthodox Church Icon of *"The Hodegetria"* revered also in the Roman Catholic Church as *"The Mother of Perpetual Help."* (For the symbolic letters see p. 139-140)

"Most Holy Theotokos, - the hope of all Christians;
shelter, - guard - and protect those,
who hope in You."

(An Orthodox Hymn from the Magnificat of Holy Day of the Presentation of our Lord). *February 2.*

In both Divine Liturgies of the next Day, Sunday, again with overflowing crowds, I announced this newest *Manifestation* to both Congregations.

Our Parishioners were thrilled to have received the added blessing of this new *Manifestation*. More than one had remarked that it had to be symbolic of the Holy Trinity. But, regardless of what explanation one could give, the fact remains that God had smiled on our beloved Parish of St. Paul's for many reasons. I truly believe this, and am so very proud to have been the founding Pastor of this Parish in 1950.

In retrospect, the many cherished years I wholeheartedly had served at St. Paul's, I consider a miracle in itself. I say this unequivocally, because I was very familiar and in communication with the life in the many Parishes of the Metropolitan New York area, and could not help but compare.

We should keep in mind though, that the Greek Orthodox Parishes before World War II were in essence Churches of the immigrants.

St. Paul's was the first Church in the Metropolitan New York area to have been organized in synchronization with the times, and on a par with the established life of the main-line Churches in America.

Consequently, it was natural that St. Paul's appealed to the young American-born couples of the Metropolitan New York area, who chose to move to Nassau County so that their family could join the St. Paul's Parish and participate in its programs.

As a result, St. Paul's was consistently being energized by the steady influx of these young families, who were vibrant with enthusiasm. In reality these young American-born parents did not have the opportunity to participate in programs in the Parishes from which they came, neither in their youth, nor as young adult parents, simply because there were none.

They loved the spirit and the new vistas charted by St. Paul's, which gave them a new outlook in their religious and social life. There was veritable family involvement.

They felt a charge that they had never sensed before. That is the reason they so willingly gave their total selves.

It became widely recognized by our Church in America, that the newly founded St. Paul's Parish had opened new vistas and was carving new paths with programs unknown in the Parishes, which our immigrant Parents had organized. There was, by common opinion, a new and vibrant contemporary spirit promoted, which lent itself to instill fiery *enthusiasm* in the St. Paul's membership.

St. Paul's gave the word *"enthusiasm"** its fullest meaning. **Everything was in God, and for God.**

Especially, I extol the virtues of the many young married couples, who had moved to Long Island from all parts of the N.Y. Metropolitan area, for a better future for their families.

For them, St. Paul's had become a haven; — a home away from home. These young couples quickly bonded in God's love through a newly founded Organization known as the "Mr. & Mrs. Club" early in the history of St. Paul's. It was the first Organization of its type in our Greek-American experience in America.

The prevailing spirit of the St. Paul's Parish brought out the best in them. This Organization very soon enveloped over 300 young couples, and gave the Parish a vitality unknown before to all its constituents and to the Community. They just couldn't do enough for their Parish.

St. Paul's had truly become a beehive of activity, with many programs to involve and satisfy the young and old alike.

---

* (The etymology of the word *"enthusiasm"* (**en Theh-OH**). comes from a composite Greek word meaning *"in God."*

Each new family was welcomed with such warmth, that they felt they had always belonged. That spirit was evident from the first days that the Parish was organized in 1950!

The Parish was founded on God's love and therefore could only head one way — forward and upward! The continuous aura of enthusiasm had never waned in the 13 years that I had the privilege to have been the spiritual head of this exemplary and unforgettable Parish.

The abundant harvest of this heart-warming and energizing enthusiasm was the construction of the ideal Parish Complex without any great benefactors, and in a relatively short period of time. It was labeled a Community "miracle." Our long established Sister Parishes in the Metropolitan New York area marveled at the spontaneous growth and all the happenings and activities associated with St. Paul's with its phenomenal progress.

Additionally, on the local level St. Paul's had also become one of the important attractions of Nassau County.

By common opinion the St.Paul's Parish Complex constitutes an adornment to Cathedral Avenue.

When the Members of St. Paul spoke with anyone, they glowed with such pride, that it sounded as if they had sole ownership of the Parish. This feeling had permeated the Community and constituted the foundation for the unparalleled and unbelievable progress. Collectively, it resulted in making the seemingly impossible, possible, — making St. Paul's a veritable reality. Did not the Lord say, that **"all things are possible to those, who believe?"** (Mark 9:23)

Faith, hope and love, the cardinal virtues had been the hallmark of the the St. Paul's Parish from day one! These three virtues were the foundation for the **"impossible to become possible."**

This indomitable spirit of the St. Paul's Membership was very obvious. It literally glowed, and repeatedly was commented upon by many of the thousands of visitors, who made the pilgrimage to revere the Icons.

Our members made the visitors feel that they too belonged! To illustrate this point, we would often see people venerate the Icons, — sit in Church for a while to pray, — then take a stroll on the gorgeously landscaped grounds, — stop in at the recreation hall for a cup of coffee and a piece of pound cake, and return once again to the Church. By their own admission, they felt so comfortable being in the uplifting spiritual environment of St. Paul's.

Our Members would be seen talking to other people as if they had known them for years. They did so much to express and maintain the effervescent spirit, easily noticed and appreciated by all. They gave the word *"welcome"* its deepest meaning. It had become "second nature" to them. Consequently, it was not unusual to see visitors over and over again, coming to venerate and to speak with our Members, as if they were old friends.

St. Paul's had established itself as a spiritual Oasis.

(From a NEWSDAY article.

PRIEST SEES FURTHER SIGNS
Confirms weeping of 3rd Icon!

A pertinent article written by Dan Foley in **NEWSDAY,** Wednesday, May 11, 1960 reads as follows after the above captions:

"A leading member of the Roman Catholic Order of the Redemptorist Fathers has confirmed the *Phenomenon* of the Weeping Madonna of Long Island and forecasts 'further Signs'!"

"The general feeling seems to be that it's a sign for us (Roman Catholic and Orthodox Churches) to get together," he commented. "A split separating the Eastern and Western Churches occurred in 1054 A.D."

The Priest is the Rev. F.J. Andres, CSSR, New York area Director of the Redemptorist Order's Perpetual Help Apostolate, which promotes devotion to the *"Mother of Perpetual Help"* and has headquarters on the Lower East Side at 173 E. 3rd Street, New York City.

PLANS REPORT

In his reference to East-West Church unity, he was calling attention to the fact that Long Island's Weeping Madonna has manifested herself in Icons in the homes of Greek Orthodox families. The Icons have been enshrined in St. Paul's Greek Orthodox Cathedral, 110 Cathedral Avenue, Hempstead, N.Y.

Fr. Andres emphasized that his visit to the Hempstead Church was only as an individual, but said he planned to report to authorities in the Redemptorist Order and would visit the Shrine again.

The Weeping Madonna is now represented in three Icons, the latest of which — a picture of the *"Mother of Perpetual Help"* — began to shed tears on Saturday.

SOMETHING BIG

After seeing the Icon late yesterday, Father Andres observed: "You can't deny the physical evidence that droplets resembling tears are coming from the picture. The interpretation of the *Phenomenon* is another thing. My personal feeling is that something big is going to come from it.

There is no Manifestation of this kind on record in the history of the *"Perpetual Help"* picture."

The Redemptorist Fathers are the guardians of the original, centuries-old *"Mother of Perpetual Help"* painting. It is in the Order's Church of St. Alphonsus Church in Rome. Father Andres presented framed copies of it to the Rev. George Papadeas, Pastor of the Hempstead Church.

"There seems to be a kind of symbolism about the succession of the Weeping Madonna Icons," the visiting Director of the Perpetual Help Apostolate noted, commenting: "The first is *'the Mother of Sorrows'* — a picture of the Western Church.

The second is *'the Mother of the Portals'* — a Byzantine picture venerated throughout the Eastern Church. The third is the *'Mother of Perpetual Help'* — which was originally an Oriental picture of the Eastern Church, but which came to the West, and was appropriated by the Western Church. I think there will be further Signs!"

STONE'S THROW

Fr. Andres was accompanied by the Rev. Joseph A. Harty, Pastor of Our Lady of Grace R.C. Church, Howard Beach, Queens, and former Pastor of the Sacred Heart R.C. Church, Island Park, L.I., where he introduced devotion to the *"Mother of Perpetual Help."*

That Church is only a stone's throw from the Catsounis home in Island Park, where the first Icon began weeping March 16.

Fr. Harty also observed the weeping of the *"Perpetual Help"* Icon in St. Paul's Church. Holding a lighted candle near the glass case containing the Icon, this writer clearly saw a flow of tears from the right eye of the Madonna's image.

The weeping of the second Icon, which had formerly been profuse, was not so apparent, but there was clearly a track from the left eye. The first Icon has not wept since March 18, 1960.

‎✣

A Recording made, but never circulated

One day I received a call from Eleni Barteri, a friend of times past. Together with her husband Steve they owned a Furniture Store. They also had one of the most popular Greek-American Radio Programs, heard by many thousands in the Metropolitan area.

I had known Steve and Eleni Barteri since the years I had served as the Assistant Priest at the Archdiocesan Cathedral (1942-1950). Eleni Barteri was a very well known singer, rendering the popular songs from Greece at the many Parish Dinner-Dances of Metropolitan New York.

She had called to tell me that she would like to come to St. Paul's to venerate the Holy Icons, and bring along a friend of the Jewish Faith, — a music composer, who was inspired by the Manifestations, and had composed a melody and lyrics about the Weeping Madonna. He had expressed to her his desire to see the Icons. I do not recall his first name, but his surname was Marcus.

They came to my office after having venerated the Holy Icons. Eleni introduced the young composer, who related to me that when he read the articles of the Weeping Icons in the Newspapers on a daily basis he was spiritually moved, and by inspiration composed a melody and lyrics to befit this *Manifestation*.

He brought the handwritten sheet of music and lyrics, offering it to St. Paul's as his gift, in honor of the Weeping Madonnas. Furthermore, he stated that any and all royalties that would ever result from any proposed recording would revert to St. Paul's.

I was very impressed by the humility and generosity of this young man. He spoke glowingly of his deep belief in God, and so reverently about the *"Sign"* of the Weeping Madonna, even though he was a practicing Hebrew.

Eleni informed me that they were in the process of scheduling the final recording session at a Studio on West 57th Street. She recognized that I was very busy, but asked if I could possibly take a few hours off to be at the Studio for the main purpose of helping to make the recording as perfect as possible. She wanted to be sure that the recording would be in proper keeping with the purpose for which it was intended.

She felt that in essence it was a religious theme and wanted the verification of a Clergyman of our Church so that the recording would be right. She further stated, that all the members of the professional choir involved in this recording through the many prior rehearsals were convinced that the record would be a great success, and more importantly a source of inspiration for many people.

I knew Eleni long enough to know that she was sincere. I too wanted to make sure that this recording would pay honor to our *"All-Holy Mother."*

Everything, regarding the Shrine at St. Paul's had been flawless so far, and I wanted to make sure that the recording, even though a private independent venture, would follow suit. I thought, that if the melody was soothing enough, it could become even popular among the young people to their advantage.

Of course, I could think this way then, because we were still living in the pre-Rock and Roll era.

The songs of that time were pleasing and soothing to the ears and to the well being.

One could appreciate the harmony of the music, as well as the ability to fully distinguish and understand the words being sung.

I feel that the Rock and Roll music which followed that era has often had a negative and I may say a soul-eroding influence on our young generation.

The appointment for the recording was set for 10:00 p.m. at a Studio in New York City. This was a totally new experience for me. I never thought a recording, for which everyone seemed so prepared could take so long! There was one cut after another in sections, until they thought the recording was presumed perfect.

But, the Producer wasn't fully satisfied. He told Eleni that the song, except for her velvety voice and the sonorous Choir singing in the background lacked something that could give it a true religious connotation. He approached me to ask if there was a hymn, or a prayer, that could be recited while the Choir would be singing Liturgical music in the background. I told him that there was such a plethora of hymns and prayers extolling the love and devotion to the Virgin Mary that it would almost be difficult to make a choice.

He also asked if it would be possible for me to make the recitation. Having personally been pleased with the soothing music and the meaningful lyrics of the recording in the making, I agreed. Not having a hymnal or prayer book with me, I translated from memory the Greek into English of a couple of Hymns dedicated to the Virgin Mary.

Hurriedly having checked my translations, I then gave them to the Producer who remarked that they were exactly what was needed to complete what he thought would be a fantastic recording. Unexpectedly, I found myself involved in the production by volunteering.

The recording without any doubt was inspirational.

It could have become a significant record, not only for the Greek Orthodox, but for all believers.

Unfortunately, as you shall see, what could have become an enormous inspirational aid, was ordered off the market the very day it was distributed to all the Music Stores and other outlets.

The song was titled: *"The Weeping Madonna."* Until this day, I cannot get over the fact that this soul-edifying record never circulated. I felt strongly that it would have had so many positive and beneficial effects.

The record commences with the Choir singing a hymn of the *"Theotokos"* from the Greek Orthodox Liturgical music in the background, while I recited the following hymn from the *"Paraklesis"* Service:

"All-Holy Mother, do not entrust me to any human protection, but accept the supplication of Your servant; for I am overcome by sorrow, and cannot bear the darts of the Demons. A wretched soul, I have no shelter, nor anywhere to seek refuge. Being attacked from all sides, I have no solace except in You. All-Holy Mother of the world, the hope and protection of the faithful, do not overlook my supplication, but grant that, which may be advantageous to me."

After this introductory recitation for the opening of the record, Eleni Barteri commenced singing:

"The Weeping Madonna."

"One night a young woman knelt in silent prayer before the image of Mary, who wore a veil around Her hair; and like a wondrous Sign from the sky,

she saw the face of the Holy Mother
with a tear in Her eye!
This story is true, they still come to view,
the Weeping Madonna, the Weeping Madonna.
Ask yourself why? Oh why did She cry?
the Weeping Madonna, the Weeping Madonna."

At this point, Eleni sang what sounded like an ending to the song, but the Choir commenced singing in the background, one of the most profound hymns in Greek, describing the beauty and merits of the Virgin Mary.

Τὴν ὡραιότητα τῆς παρθενίας σου καὶ τὸ ὑπέρλαμπρὸν τὸ τῆς ἁγνείας σου ὁ Γαβριὴλ καταπλαγείς, ἐβόα σοι, Θεοτόκε. Ποῖόν σοι ἐγκώμιον προσαγάγω ἐπάξιον· τί δὲ ὀνομάσω σε; ἀπορῶ καὶ ἐξίσταμαι· διό, ὡς προσετάγην, βοῶ σοι· Χαῖρε, ἡ Κεχαριτωμένη.

The translation is:

"Astounded by the comeliness of Your Virginity, and the exceeding splendor of Your purity, Gabriel cried out to You, the Theotokos: 'What hymn worthy of praise, can I present to You? How shall I address you? I am at a loss and stand in astonishment. Wherefore, as commanded, I cry out unto You: Rejoice! the One, who is blessed with Grace'."

While the Choir was singing this hymn as a background, I recited the following hymn:

"Open the portals of Your compassion O Blessed Theotokos, so that hoping in You, we shall not fail; through You, we are delivered from adversities, for through You is the salvation of the genus of Christians."

When the recitation was finished, Eleni again sang the refrain:

> "Ask yourself why?
> Oh why did she cry?
> The Weeping Madonna,
> The Weeping Madonna."

At the end of the recording Eleni held the final note while the Choir commenced to build up the final crescendo, for a grand harmonious ending. Indeed, it was and is, a most inspiring recording, which I have treasured over all the past years, listening to it from time to time.

I was happy that Mrs. Barteri had asked that I attend the recording session to make sure that it would be flawless religiously. And it was. I really had no idea that I would be asked to contribute by reciting a couple of our age-old hymns, — in essence prayers, in English translation, to give a fuller meaning to the recording.

But, as with many instances in life so difficult to comprehend, no one knows what forces may be at work covertly to terminate, destroy, or nullify some worthy project.

All during the possibly perfect and most uplifting period experienced at St. Paul's during the last three months, — a period laden with spirituality, — without any forewarning one day, I received a Western Union Telegram from Archbishop Iakovos which literally shocked me. He was ordering me to bring the 3 Holy Icons to the Archdiocese.

Still further he had ordered, that the new recording be withdrawn from the market immediately.

How, and in what manner His Eminence had been informed regarding the recording, I'll never know. Lord knows, of how negatively the whole matter must have been presented to him.

I had received the telegram only a few days after the recording session in the Studio, and was totally surprised that the record was already on the market, and furthermore that my name was included.

I felt as if lightning had struck close to home. At a complete loss to comprehend the matter from any aspect I showed the telegram to the few St. Paul Council Members, who on a rotation basis were serving on that day to accommodate in various ways the thousands who visited the Church daily.

They were equally dumbfounded, as well as feeling offended by the news. Initially the Council Members were not inclined to moving the Icons to the Archdiocese, but I explained to them that we had to comply. I called both the Catsounis and Koulis families to apprise them of the Archbishop's demands.

The Catsounis couple said that they had donated the Icon to the Church, having even signed the back, and that it was their insistent wish, that the Icon would not be moved, but to stay in St. Paul's Cathedral in perpetuity.

Peter and Antonia Koulis submitted to the demands of His Eminence to have the *"Portaitissa"* Icon taken to the Archdiocese, but requested and did receive from the Archbishop the *"Mother of Perpetual Help"* Icon which had been given to them, after they had donated the *"Portaitissa"* to St. Paul's.

It was impossible at that time to get through to His Eminence to ask him what the reason was for his impulsive act. I could have answered any questions that he must have had in his mind.

I felt strongly and still do, that we had done justice to the Manifestations having accorded all possible honor, respect and dignity. Everything was always kept, as it should be, on the highest plane. This was my primary concern.

My every thought and move was to be worthy of the great honor brought to our Parish through the blessings of the *"Divine Signs."*

With all the hundreds of thousands of pilgrims, there was never even the slightest incident, that would have marred the beautiful spiritual picture of St. Paul's.

By nature, I was always conscious of my complete dedication to all matters pertaining to the life and interest of the Church over the many years of my Priesthood, which speak for themselves. That is why this new, unexpected demand was so enigmatic.

Finally I was able to get through to one of the Archbishop's assistants and was informed of the alleged *"commercialization"* through a poster that was hung on the front window of Woolworth's in Times Square. It was supposedly not befitting the dignity of the Church showing me blessing Eleni Barteri while she was venerating the Icon at St. Paul's.

I lost no time in driving over an hour to Times Square. Having asked to see the Manager of Woolworth's, I explained to him that I had no understanding of, and would never have granted permission of my appearing on any commercial poster.

Therefore, I asked him to please remove it, which he did in my presence. In the meantime he mentioned to me that it was an inspiring and unusual recording, and that the demand for the record far exceeded his supply on the first day having been a complete sellout. This was understandable, because the articles on the Weeping Madonna were daily seen in the Newspapers and over TV. People had a sincere interest for anything pertaining to the *Manifestations.*

After leaving Woolworth's I visited Steve and Eleni Barteri at their business to inform them of what had transpired.

They were completely stunned by this unbelievable action and deeply apologetic to me, never having envisioned that any such situation could ever have arisen, especially since they knew of my complete dedication to the Church.

I told them, as they very well knew, that my involvement with the record was not pre-planned. It was only to help as much as I could in the recording production to guarantee, as it were, religious feeling and significance, which would be an aid to the spiritual uplifting of the people. This was a given fact. I had signed no paper, had no involvement, nor had given anyone permission to use my picture or name.

Finally I requested the Barteris to contact the producer and inform him accordingly to stop the production of records. They promised that they would closely monitor the situation with every possible immediate action. I must emphasize, that they felt badly for me, but I felt doubly bad for them, because they had not only invested substantially to make the recording, but they really believed that this record would have served as a great uplift to those who would hear it.

Thus, with the removal of the two Icons, my vision for the construction of a separate Shrine dedicated to the *"All-Holy Mother,"* on the grounds of St. Paul, utterly vanished.

Truly, — until this day — I have never gotten over it, nor ever will. I simply have never understood the reasoning behind this sudden action.

I strongly felt, that there must have been some other way for this matter to have been handled, so that everything would have been kept intact, and not bring to an abrupt ending to what had become a spiritual Oasis for so many thousands, who sought spiritual refreshment!

Our whole Parish, though thoroughly disappointed by this unforeseen action, has never lost the feeling imbedded in their hearts from the blessings, which had been felt through the *"Divine Signs,"* and all the related Events.

The whole Parish truly believed, that the blessings which had come from *Above* were indescribable, and constituted inspiring special gifts of the spirit.

Very deeply I believe, that these Blessings had come to all people, but especially to our blessed Parish of St. Paul's. They had definitely left their indelible marks in our hearts, forever to be treasured.

Thirty six years after the *Manifestations,* — that is in 1996, Archbishop Iakovos prior to his retirement, returned the Icon of the *"Portaitissa"* to the St. Paul's Cathedral. The third Icon, that is *"The Hodegetria,"* or *"Mother of Perpetual Help,"* was given by Archbishop Iakovos to Mr. & Mrs. Peter Koulis at the time the two Icons were taken to the Archdiocese at his request in the summer of 1960, and was kept in their family. Presently it is in the possession of their daughter Bessie.

Preparing to write this Book I did contact Bessie, who informed me that her father had passed away years before she bade farewell to her mother in 1990. According to her information it was significant for her, that at the time of her mother's passing the Icon stopped tearing after the many years!

She sent me a picture of the Icon (next page), which having shed tears for about twenty five years, had resulted in the paper Icon practically being melted, where the stream of tears had formed tracks from the tears.

But, thanks to Peter and Pagona Catsounis gift of the first Icon, a small Grotto was built inside the St. Paul's Cathedral with only the *"Mother of Sorrows,"* the first of the three tearing Icons, enshrined. Daily, people come from all over to pray and light a candle at this Shrine.

This Shrine is the only visible Sign in the St. Paul's Parish when God had sent us His Blessings so abundantly through the three Weeping Icons of the *"All-Holy Mother."*

The effect of tearing over the many years, shows vividly on the lithographed print of *"The Hodegetria."*-*"Mother of Perpetual Help."*

Each year on the Anniversary date of the first *"Divine Sign,"* there is a special Celebration at the St. Paul's Cathedral during which the *"Paraklesis"* Service is prayed.

At the 28th Annual Commemoration on March 16, 1988 held at St. Paul's, Pagona Catsounis had composed and read the following poem in Greek.

I translated it from the Greek, but understandably, not able to achieve the proper poetic meter in English, my translation is in prose.

✳

My Prayer to the *"Panagia"*

Our most sweet *"Panagia,"* we know that Your arms are always outstretched to lovingly embrace us.

In our trials and tribulations, — it is You who gives us comfort; — it is You, who comes to our aid to bolster our faith!

The beauty of all the flowers upon the earth are reflected in Your countenance, as are the prayers of the faithful, which fill the air like the beauty and fragrance of rose petals.

In Your affectionate bosom, the suffering find comfort and strength. They feel protected by Your warm and loving grace; — Your grace is a veritable Beacon, always guiding us safely to port.

In every sadness, sorrow and grief — in every tear drop, wound and pain -- it is You, our most beloved and revered *"Panagia,"* who rushes to our side, to comfort and to heal us.

Our *"Family Altar,"* adorned with Your Holy Icon,— the flickering flame of the vigil light, — and the fragrance of the incense from the censer,— all these combine to reflect and radiate Your love and ever-presence amongst us all.

We too — Your loving children are ever so happy to always offer to You, our revered Mother a bouquet of our love.

How truly happy we become, and how very pleasing it is to our ears, when we hear the sweet melodies of gratitude coming from the souls, who have been healed by Your intercessions.

Our most sweet *"Panagia;"* we revere You through Your Holy Icon. We ask, that You receive us all, Your faithful and humble servants in the warmth of Your affectionate bosom.

Stretch forth Your Blessed hand, and grant Your healing to the many suffering souls, oh my sweet *"Panagia!"*

Pagona Catsounis
March 1988

A Spiritual Link
to the *"Divine Signs"*

By the year 1960, I was already a Priest for 18 years. Aside from my Parish activities, I was often assigned to various missions by the Archbishop, which took me to Greece and other Countries in the Middle East.

While on these missions, I always made it a point to visit various Shrines, most of which, were dedicated to the Virgin Mary.

Also, through my reading I had become familiar with the numerous centuries-old Monasteries and Shrines in Greece, where Miracles had happened by Divine blessing.

The most renowned of these is the Church of the *"Panagia"* on the Island of Tenos. On the Anniversary of the very Holy Day of the *"Dormition of the Theotokos,"* August 15th, it is estimated that over 30,000 faithful converge on this small Island to venerate the Holy Icon; — some hoping to be cured, and others to find solace for their soul. Many hundreds of Greek Orthodox Americans make the Pilgrimage each year to venerate the Holy Icon there.

Tenos is to the Greek Orthodox, what the Lady of Lourdes is to the Roman Catholics.

Over the years I had heard of, and read in the Greek Press of Miracles happening on the Holy Day of the *"Dormition of the Theotokos"* in Tenos; these Miracles are attested and documented during this Annual Holy Day.

The Shrine in Tenos had been designated as one of the highlights of the two religious and cultural Pilot Programs sponsored by the Greek Orthodox Archdiocese of America. These Programs were to be an experiment to ascertain if our Greek-American children could adapt in a Camping program thousands of miles away from their home.

These Pilot Programs of 1961 and 1962 would determine the feasibility of constructing our own Facility in Greece to accommodate our Young Greek Americans for a month in our own Quarters. The Archdiocese believed, that by participating in a concentrated and well planned cultural, educational and religious program, our youth would be permanently influenced for their whole life.

They would be imbued, not only with the culture of the ancient Greek civilization, but also by their pilgrimage to the Religious Sites hallowed by the Apostles St. Andrew and St. Paul.

I was honored to have been chosen to lead the first group of the two Pilot programs scheduled for Greece, in the summer of 1961.

Thirty seven teenage boys and girls from all parts of the United States boarded the S.S. Frederica for the 11 day voyage over the Atlantic Ocean and Mediterranean Sea, to become the month-long guests at the Camp of the Commercial Bank of Greece, and that of the Bank of Greece.

The boys bunked at the Camp of the Commercial Bank, and the girls at the Camp of the Bank of Greece. The daily activities lasting into the late evening were in common.

After the day's activities there was the parting to the respective Camps. Again in the morning, our youth would rejoin company for the activities of the day, which included tours to the Ancient Archeological Sites, as well as to the Christian monuments from St. Paul's time. Also included in the program, as mentioned, was a cruise on the beautiful Aegean Sea, to take us to our *"All-Holy Mother's"* Shrine on the Island of Tenos.

I am very proud that this program met with complete success. Our youth quickly responded favorably in adapting to summer camping in Greece and returned to America very spirited.

The following summer in 1962, the second and final program was a duplication of the first and met with equal success. I am thankful, that my grown teenagers were part of this second Pilot program. Because of their previous experience from the initial one in 1961, they were able to give valuable needed assistance.

Among the 40 Campers of the second group in 1962 was a young boy from Danville, Virginia about 13 years old. This youngster's glasses had such thick prism lenses, that without them he could have been declared legally blind. His grandmother in Danville had prepared him psychologically for his Pilgrimage to Tenos.

She had repeatedly told him to believe with all his heart and all his mind, and pray to the *"Panagia,"* to intercede for his vision to be cured.

He was to wash his face and eyes with water from the miraculous spring in the Grotto beneath the Church and pray with all his heart. The youngster went to Greece with a very positive note. He was spiritually girded and was eagerly looking forward to the pilgrimage to Tenos.

This miracle, for which many prayed, did come to pass. Standing in front of the Grotto in prayer, the young Camper from Danville, Va. took off his glasses at the spring remembering his Grandmother's admonition. With all the resources of faith and love that a 13 year old could possibly have in his heart, he washed his eyes thoroughly.

The moment was instantaneous! He immediately saw before him bright light almost like a blinding flash. The haziness he had known and lived with all his life, bordering on darkness, was dispelled.

Spontaneously, after having washed his eyes, he shouted with exhilaration, and commenced jumping up and down shouting: *"I see, I see!"* After blessing himself in gratitude with the sign of the Cross, a visible act of prayer for all Orthodox, his first act was to throw his glasses at his feet and jump on them to destroy them forever.

His fellow Campers equally participating in this inexpressible joy, with tear-filled eyes joined in the jumping, exclaiming and hugging the fellow Camper and each other.

Their tears of joy ran like the miraculous spring before them. This effervescent joy was also shared by many pilgrims from all parts of Greece, who were standing in line to have their turn at the spring.

The Priest of the Shrine Fr. Eleftherios was summoned. After having seen the young lad, and hearing the testimony of fellow Campers he gave the order for the Church bells to toll, a signal to the residents of Tenos that a Miracle had taken place. The young Camper from Danville subsequently was taken to the Island's Ophthalmologist, who examined him.

After examining the boy's eyes the Doctor stated, that while he did not know his previous history, his vision now was 20/20. One can easily imagine the indescribable and lasting joy, not only of the blessed young boy who was cured, but also that of all his fellow Campers.

The success of the two experimental programs of our youth adapting for a camping program in Greece set the wheels in motion for the Archdiocese to build our own Facility to our specifications.

Eight years later, in 1970 our Summer Camping Facility was ready to receive its first group of campers. I was privileged to have been sent by Archbishop Iakovos to organize and direct the opening program of the Archdiocesan Camp, the *"Ionian Village."*

Built on the beautiful shores of the Ionian Sea as a permanent installation, it resembles a first class resort.

It was in June 1970, when the 30 Counselors, a Doctor and a Nurse escorting 300 youngsters, became the charter campers of the *"Ionian Village."*

Along with the varied duties of such an ambitious undertaking, especially during the first session, I didn't foresee the deluge of calls from the Grecian relatives of our Campers, who were apprised by their own in America. and wanted to host the youngsters in their respective city or village.

It is easily understood, how these relatives of our campers were thrilled at the prospect of seeing and hosting their young relatives. They were calling to make possible arrangements to receive their young relatives in their respective city or village.

The requests came from the very first day of our arrival. I knew well, that this would create a tremendous problem, as well as expose our Campers unnecessarily to some possible accident outside the Camp, over which we would have had no control. It would be problematic and risky from any aspect. More importantly, it would interfere with our concentrated, religious and educational program.

Therefore, a policy had to be established. After discussing this thoroughly with the committee, it was decided that no camper could travel outside the Camp to visit relatives. The relatives had to make the trip from all parts of

Greece, if they wanted to visit any camper. Furthermore, in order that our daily activities would not be hindered, the visits of the relatives were set for Sunday afternoons only. I personally took the responsibility to come in contact with the visiting relatives, to check credentials etc.

On one occasion, speaking to a group of relatives who had come to the Camp to visit with their relative, I happened to mention that the *"Ionian Village"* came into being as a result of the two successful Pilot programs in 1961 and 1962.

Much to my surprise, a relative of a camper from our group having heard this, told me that she was present near a group of young campers from America, when she had visited the Grotto in Tenos in 1962. She said that she witnessed the healing of one of these youngsters, who was miraculously cured, after washing his eyes and drinking from the spring of the Grotto.

It was surprising, and so pleasing for me to have heard this added testimony from a native of Greece, who personally had witnessed the *Miracle* in Tenos of one of our 1962 Campers, and to have vividly remembered it after so many years! You know the saying: *"It's a small world!"*

When this lady mentioned the *Miracle,* my mind spontaneously flashed back to St. Paul's and the *Manifestations.* In a flash my thoughts mentally connected me with the inspiring experiences at St. Paul's in Hempstead, Long Island ten years before.

I am so thankful that I had the opportunity to have visited many Shrines in Greece. For me, they are veritable spiritual Oases. My visits to them have always left me refreshed and very uplifted. It was to me, like being as thirsty as one could be in a desert, — then suddenly, coming upon an oasis to drink the crystal clear, refreshing, cool water.

That is the nature of the spiritual springs or fountains, whether they be a Shrine, or a Monastery; they refresh us because they are constantly tuned in to God and His Glory.

That was the captivating picture, which was experienced at St. Paul's during the blessed months of the *Manifestations* in 1960.

Unless one visits any of these spiritual Oases, it is difficult to explain the feelings, which overwhelm and humble a person. There is something indescribable in their atmosphere. It is readily understandable, because it is there, where we are removed from the vicissitudes of life, — from the everyday mundane and temporal affairs, and for some precious moments we are able to sense an inner peace, — completely soul-nourishing and fulfilling.

In such Oases, the chief involvement is communicating and communion with God. Without a doubt, the feelings sensed, as well as the emotions felt, far exceed any words, or poetic descriptions,— no matter how eloquent.

Having then visited a few of these Shrines over the years — years before the tearing Icon of Island Park, I would often think to myself, ***"why is it that we, here in America, had never experienced a "Sign from Above," as has happened in many parts of Greece and the Middle East which are spotted with Shrines?"***

I would assume that *"Signs from Above"* may have also appeared in other Countries, about which I am not familiar. After all, God is the Father of all people.

But, I had always felt, that some *"Sign,"* some miracle from *"Above"* of a tangible nature, would greatly serve to further bolster the faith of the people, and give them spiritual comfort. This thought crossed my mind so many times over many years.

Lo, and behold! Here we were in the Spring of 1960!

Little could I ever have envisioned or imagined, that my inward thought and hope of many years would become substance; and specifically here, within the blessed environment of our great Family at St. Paul's!

The Good Lord had chosen to extend His beneficent Hand of Grace to bless the believers as well as to awaken many from their spiritual lethargy. The means would happen in a very simple, yet most powerful manner, — through small lithographed Icons; — a *"Sign"* which no less would confound those, who are not prone to believing!

I humbly state, that this could not have happened to a more deserving Parish, where love and harmony were systematically cultivated from its inception, and as a result bring to fruition one of the finest Parishes, not only in the Greater N.Y. area, but of the whole East Coast.

As I stated, — I also repeat now, — that which I firmly believe, — that it was God, placing His Seal on the blessed work for His Glory, which was systematically cultivated and being accomplished through His love at St. Paul's, in such a brief period of time.

❋

The N. Y. NEWSDAY, 30 Years Later

"The reporting on the Icons very much alive in NEWSDAY article after 30 years."

I have been blessed by still maintaining contact with many of my beloved Parishioners at Saint Paul's, sealed with an everlasting friendship to this day, after having left St.Paul's in 1963 to be assigned as the Dean of the Archdiocesan Cathedral in New York.

I reminisce, reading their letters, and file the clip-pings which they periodically send me regarding events about St. Paul's.

A few years ago, a Parishioner had sent me an article from the **NEW YORK NEWSDAY.**

As is my practice, I placed this in my file, to which one day I would refer, when I would commence writing this Book on the 40th Anniversary Year of the *Manifestations*. It was not only significant, but very important for me to have received this particular clipping, and to read that:

"NEWSDAY had included the Weeping Icon, as one of the most memorable Events of the past 50 years!"

This was a very just recognition of the *"Divine Signs"* by a major New York Newspaper.

The date of the clipping was October 14, 1990, pre-cisely thirty and one half years after the Holy Icons had shed tears, and referred to in the original article of April 13, 1960.

The article, reported by Mr. Jim Hadjin was captioned:

"Reporter Sees Icon Weep."

In a sub-title, the following was mentioned: **"If the rescue of Benny Hooper in the '50s was a figurative mira-cle, the weeping Icon of the '60s became a literal miracle to many of its witnesses.** One of them was the reporter Jim Hadjin, who had to convince some highly skeptical Editors to get his account into the paper."

The article as reported then by Jim Hadjin in part, read as follows:

"I saw tears welling in the eyes of a lithograph of the Virgin Mary yesterday — teardrops, that glistened in the flickering light cast by a small candle. Someone pulled the candle away and the flat light of the afternoon sun streaming through a window confirmed that it was no illusion."

"It was an 8 by 10 inch, glass-framed picture of the Virgin Mary wearing a red shawl and holding in her left arm the Christ Child."

"My eye was led to a bleeding wound on the right cheek of the Virgin, but was immediately arrested.

The wound and drops of blood were painted. But, just to the right of the red-painted drops were two parallel wet streaks running vertically from the Virgin's eyes down to the bottom edge of the painting under the glass."

"A closer look showed that there was a drop of clear liquid, apparently water, at the corner of each eye and that the painted eyes were swollen from the dampness. Tiny droplets were spaced along the rivulets leading to the bottom edge, and the cardboard margin at the bottom of the painting was obviously liquid-stained. No liquid was visible any-where else on the painting."

"Later, after the **NEW YORK NEWSDAY** Staff - photographer Jim Nightingale had taken photographs of the lithograph, the Rev. George Papadeas, Pastor of St. Paul's Greek Orthodox Church picked up the wood-framed painting and turned it over. While I watched, he bent out the metal clips that held a cardboard backing sheet loosely in place, removed the sheet and placed it aside.

He then lifted the lithograph far away from the glass, so that I could see that the painting itself was glued on another piece of cardboard about the thickness of a notebook cover."

"The lithographed sheet felt smooth to the touch — like non-porous, silky paper. At the top, about an inch of that sheet was folded back over the cardboard and glued down.

Except for that minute added thickness at the top, the joined sheets — lithograph and cardboard — had no bulges and were of uniform thickness throughout. Aside from the stain on the bottom margin, there were no liquid stains on the cardboard backing. There apparently was nothing there, that could have produced any liquid."

"I examined the painting several times during the more than two hours that I was in the apartment. The drops could not actually be seen moving downward."

"But on first examination, there was a full drop in the corner of each eye. Shortly before Father Papadeas removed the back cover, those drops appeared to be below the eyes and seemed to have diminished in size, and the eyes themselves looked glistening damp and swollen. Shortly after he had reframed the painting, I and those around me saw a fresh drop well in each eye."

(End of the NEWSDAY article)
❊

Some Voices are heard after 40 Years

To be sure, here in America, we may have not had the opportunity to have viewed the original Icon of the *"Portaitissa,"* only because it is zealously kept in the Iveron Monastery. But, we had an inexpensive lithographed copy of the *"Portaitissa"* on Long Island, through which hundreds of thousands witnessed the *"Divine Signs."* Actual tears had emanated from the eyes of the *"Panagia,"* the *"All-Holy Mother"* of all.

I believe, that through this very simple medium, God, in His Omniscience and Omnipotence designated the *"Sign"* of the tearing Icons for the primary purpose of working miracles in the hearts of people in our troubled times.

God continues to speak to us, but while *"we have ears to hear we do not hear, and while we have eyes to see, we do not see."* (Mark 8:18)

While there are numerous Shrines in Greece and the Middle East dedicated to the *"Panagia,"* which in themselves could be the subject of more than one book, my purpose for this Book was to relate the Manifestation of the *"Divine Signs"* as they came in our midst, as well as to connect these *"Signs"* to various related historical facts.

These *"Signs"* constituted a true blessing from *Above* for hundreds of thousands of pilgrims in 1960, and even for millions throughout the believing world, but was felt in depth by my unforgettable Parish of St. Paul's in Hempstead.

Over the years I have received calls from my Parishioner-Friends, who would write to me when they would see a film clip of the *"Divine Signs,"* or a mention of the Weeping Madonnas. Also, when they saw Newspaper feature articles about Miracles and Supernatural Phenomena, which included our Holy Icons they would send these articles to me.

Receiving these news items over the past decades further fortified my feeling, that the Events of the Weeping Madonnas were deeply imbedded in so many hearts and minds. This pleased me very much. For those, who were blessed to revere the Miraculous Icons, this would constitute a life-long memory and blessing.

Planning to write this Book, I thought it would be fitting to hear from a few of my former Parishioners and Friends over the years, with whom I have not lost contact since I was re-assigned from St. Paul's 37 years ago. I would ask them to reply through a brief questionnaire, as having been eye-witnesses of the *"Divine Signs,"* and of their involvement as hosts to the hordes of Pilgrims that passed through St. Paul's.

I feel sure that these Parishioners of St. Paul's generally represent the feelings of all their contemporary fellow Parishioners, who were present when the *Manifestations* happened in 1960.

I had posed questions, asking them to concisely express what they felt when they first saw the tearing Icons of the *"All-Holy Mother"* — what effect these had on them, as well as on the Parishioners in general, and what their feelings are today, after 40 years!

I further asked them if I could use their names after they completed the questionnaire. Without exception they all requested that their names be withheld, but they were very happy to fill in the paragraphs on the sheets I had sent to them. This questionnaire was by no means an inclusive list, but also not exclusive.

When I received the completed questionnaires, I wasn't surprised that their answers ran pretty much in the same vein. This was only natural, because I had witnessed 40 years ago the general and similar effect that the *Manifestations* had on our Membership at the time that they happened.

Below are some of the feelings expressed:

Feelings of 40 years ago, now recalled by Members of the Saint Paul's Parish

— — **"It was, as we say, *'unbelievable!'*** I said to myself, that this was not happening in some remote village in Europe, but here in my Church! What a humbling experience! The question *'why?'* kept popping up in my head.

But as I said it was a humbling experience and we were taking part in seeing a Sign thrust before us, — **was it a 'wake-up call'?"**

— — **"I have always been a Church-goer,** devoted to my Greek Orthodox Faith, but the *Manifestations* instilled a renewed feeling in me and my Family regarding worship, reverence, faith and the power of prayer.

I was witnessing an unbelievable, awe-inspiring Divine moment that will never be forgotten. — I saw for myself the tears of the *"Panagia"* — the Weeping Madonna. I can still see and feel that sacred moment of the veneration of our Holy Mother, and sense the chills traveling up my spine.

Our *"All-Holy Mother"* has always been very close to my heart! Most vividly I remember the three white doves in formation all the way from Island Park to St. Paul's and their flying around the dome for the duration of the three hour Service."

— — **"It was the most incredible thing to see.** Although I know there were some skeptics, I think it was a positive experience. I remember people's discussions trying to figure out what the message was being sent to us. It was something that has stayed with me all my life. It strengthened my faith, and still being a part of St. Paul's, it is a beautiful legacy that we have given our children."

— — **"I was amazed because of the stream of tears** from the Madonna's eyes flowing exactly as they would on any weeping person. It was unquestionably a deep religious experience, but one which left many mystified regarding the significance of the Weeping Icon."

— — **"We were overwhelmed with emotion,** and felt humble at the sight of the Weeping Madonna. We know that it brought us closer to the Church and to each other."

— — **"I'll never forget the Archbishop's words** when he spoke on the night he had come to the Koulis home. The words still ring in my ears: *'The Holy Mother wept for the non-believers to believe!'* I was happy that I was present and do believe deeply, although I must confess, that not having seen the first Icon tearing, I was then a kind of a doubting Thomas."

— — **"With my Family we closely followed all the Events** at the Koulis home and at St. Paul's hosting the multitudes, that continuously converged to see the Miracle. While assisting the people in line I had occasion to observe and witness their feelings, which brought them to tears. Observing the humility of our Parishioners, my feelings became deeper and deeper."

— — **"We lived in Flushing at the time of the Icons.** I was in the last days of my pregnancy. My devotion to our *"All-Holy Mother"* has always been great with gratitude.

Normally it was wrong to travel all that distance to St. Paul's, when it was within hours of my due date. But I felt a strong impulse to come to St. Paul's to pray before the Icon. I am so happy that I did. I felt so fulfilled, and had faith that nothing would happen to me. No sooner had I returned home, than I was rushed to the Hospital and prepared for a C-Section, which gave us a gorgeous baby girl. I thank the Good Lord and His Holy Mother for all and in all."

The remarks of the 3 previous pages were from a small representative cross section of St. Paul's, who personally lived the experience 40 years ago.

✳   ✳   ✳

Now, 40 years later, the same people recall so lovingly those unforgettable days

Now, 40 years later, these same People express their present feelings

— — **"The thoughts are still with me.** Living now in Florida, I recently came across a picture of St. Paul's in an Archdiocesan Sunday School Book. I showed it to a young mother standing near me, who said: *'Tell us about the Weeping Icons. You were there. What a neat story'."*

— — **"Personally I feel that perhaps the 3 Icons** were forewarning us of coming events, especially the deaths of

relate those most precious moments in her life and in the history of St. Paul's.

"I often wondered why did these *Manifestations* happen in our Parish. I believe that St. Paul's being a young and progressive Parish with a complete cross-section of the population, composed of intelligent forward looking Parishioners, of professional and business people, blue collar workers etc., needed a vehicle to transmit this to the world at large.

Also the instrument to communicate, and do what it takes to transmit these happenings. Our Priest had all the qualities to have accomplished this. He was a Priest who persevered and saw things through. I often wondered where he got all that energy that he constantly expended."

— — **"What a wonderful labor of love to write this Book** 40 years later. I was only 6 when the Miracle occurred — but I remember well my mother's reaction — the tears, the prayers, the veneration of the Icon of the *"Panagia."* This Event became more and more meaningful to me as I matured and learned more about our Faith.

As a matter of fact only last year I asked Pagona Catsounis regarding her experience, and listening to her sent chills up and down my spine.

I also remember, that when I was a student at the Sacred Heart Academy, a few blocks down from St. Paul's, the Nuns would ask me about the *"Panagia"* and to relate the story. On several occasions we had "field trips" to St. Paul's, and I was so proud to show my Church and the Icons to my classmates.

I truly believe, that it was so fitting for this Event to occur in the home of Pagona Catsounis. She is a very sweet, devout and beautiful individual. She encompasses so many virtues which make her outstanding and a most deserving individual."

"Why Did She Cry?"

"Why did She cry?" was the question, which every-one must have asked themselves or others during the *Manifestations*. Understandably, it is the most natural question regarding the tearing of the three Holy Icons of our *"All-Holy Mother, St. Mary the Ever-Virgin."* These *Manifestations* have been declared *"Divine Signs"* by the Ecumenical Patriarchate.

"Why did She cry?" In reply, — one can speculate and come up with various answers, depending on personal perception and the depth of their faith. But, for the believing Christian it is a matter of introspection, which will help him/her to understand why these *Manifestations* came to us through the Icons of our *"All-Holy Mother"* shedding tears in 1960; and significantly for these to have happened within the relatively small geographical area of the St. Paul's Greek Orthodox Parish in Hempstead, Long Island.

During the last couple of generations, and especially the last one, a diametrically opposite picture of what existed previously has evolved.

It wasn't that there were no problems or troubles in days past, — but a greater measure of respect and self-respect was enjoyed, as compared with that of recent years.

As of the last generation or so, it is apparent that the Eternal Values have been diluted to the point that they are practically irrelevant.

Thus, we have become morally flabby as compared to the days of old, when respect for the eternal, lasting values had kept us strong within the Family, the Community and the Nation.

In today's world, for too many people, nothing of true and lasting value seems to be important, and nothing seems to matter anymore, unless it is allied with something of material value, — or has to do with *"self."*

Unfortunately, to a great extent it really has become a *"me"* generation. — *"So what!"* *"Whatever!"* are the dismissing responses we hear, even when it pertains to very serious matters!

The lofty ideals of God and Country appear to be outmoded, and many seem so unconcerned. Statistics though, have proven that our youth, and by extension our Country, has negatively been affected since that one atheist in 1963, Madalyn Murray O'Hair was able to out-voice the 250,000,000 Citizens of our Country! Incidentally you may have read that she suddenly and mysteriously disappeared a couple of years ago.

Imagine, — one woman, — an avowed atheist, being successful in banning prayer from the Schools! Nine Supreme Court Justices rendered the decision in her favor to effect this! The silent majority of our Country remained just that — silent, — not voicing collectively their opinion.

My personal opinion is, that there should have been a public referendum for such a basic and vital issue, since it directly affected the majority. I believe, that if there had been a referendum, prayers would still be offered in our Schools for the benefit of all, as was the Country-wide experience over a generation ago. Continuously we read in the Papers that efforts for prayers in public schools and gatherings are put forth only to be squelched by opposite forces.

I was in the graduating class of 1,002 Seniors in the Altoona High School in 1937. I recall so very easily even until today, after 65 years, that one of the lasting memories which has remained with me was the morning assembly in the Auditorium, pledging our allegiance to our Flag, hearing a reading from the Psalms and singing religious-theme songs like *"Come Thou Almighty King ....."*

Everyone, — the Faculty and Students of all Faiths, — Christians and non-Christians alike participating. The bulk of elder Americans know this, because it was the unquestioned practice in all the Schools of our Country.

In my four years in High School, there was never a single complaint of discrimination or objection registered, and I feel confident, that this must have been the case in all the Schools of our Country. Why did all this change diametrically, so as to have affected our Country so negatively?

If those against prayers in Schools a generation ago were sizeable groups around the Country, militantly marching for their cause, perhaps it might have been somewhat understood at that time. But, when they were so very few, unnoticed and insignificant for the most part, represented by Madalyn Murray O'Hair, this becomes impossible to comprehend! Where was democracy?

In retrospect, I often think, how could this ever have happened in our God-fearing Country, founded on trust in God, and for whose advantage? If anything, I think that prayers in the Schools were an edifying and a powerful force which served to bring people together.

Today especially, so many of our young people do not receive any information, exposure, or instruction about God and the Bible. Thus, with no code for their moral undergirding we all suffer the consequences.

If we had prayers in our Schools, these young people would at least have occasion to hear of God and the Bible so as to have a moral compass in life.

What a blessing it would be to have a return to those days, which of course is nothing short of a dream. Our Society would be so much the richer for it, and I believe that our youth would be more contained But, how could this ever be possible, when the silent majority seems to always be intimidated by the very vocal minority, whose voice is the only one heard? — Most unfortunate.

The Presidency, as well as the Supreme Court held in such high esteem a generation ago, unfortunately have fallen from their pedestal, devoid of the respect always accorded them by the American People.

Our Representatives in Washington usually deal with the physical counterpart of humans, without much attention to the spiritual. Religion is a word to avoid, in order that the minority is not intimidated. After all, has it not been drilled into us that we have complete separation of Church and State? This has been worked to death!

Separation of Church and State is very wise and should hold. It is understandable that the State cannot espouse any Church. But we seem to forget, that our Great Nation was founded on religious principles with a strong faith in God, and that prayers until *"yesterday"* were said in Schools, public functions, political gatherings etc. without question.

One by one though, these are slowly evaporating because the majority is intimidated by a rip-tide of a very small minority.

Some of our elected Leaders, who supposedly represent us in Government seem to be more concerned with the possibility of losing votes if they were to take a stand on some important issue.

That is why we desperately need a return to government by principles, instead of having a government by politics.

Also, we have projected the 20th Century as the age of unprecedented progress. We hear it all the time whether in the social field, the technological, the scientific, the economic, or what have you!

We emphasize and boast about the great progress we have achieved and our great discoveries. But, we neglect to mention the great cost to humans, and the rampant unhappiness this progress has brought to those, who have labored strenuously to attain this *"progress!"* The cost and damage to many people responsible for this progress is inestimable.

Would you disagree, that many of the people involved in this *"progress,"* laboring under constant stress to achieve, are basically unhappy and unfulfilled?

For so many people, the goal of making *"lots of money"* — becoming rich, or the gaining a position of fame and worldly *"glory"* seem to be the primary objective. Those who choose to set such goals, are often oblivious to the fact, that the goal they set out to pursue, perhaps may have to be realized at the expense of their spiritual counterpart! This fact seems to be of little concern to them. Many have forgotten that we are composed of soul and body, and it is the soul, which is eternal.

The reasoning may be that the spirit, or soul deals with *"intangibles,"* whereas the physical and the material deal in *"tangibles,"* and therefore it is only the tangibles which have the potential to fuel their worldly goal! And, if it does happen that they are successful in achieving their set goal, we can almost be sure, that generally they will probably be serving mainly one person, — *self!*

Greed is the name of the game. Too many are out there using every unscrupulous means to get to the top, disregarding and nullifying every moral fibre, which is implanted naturally in all hearts.

If only time was taken to think on the Lord's words, and then work at giving them implementation, there is no question that we personally would be happier, and living in a much better world. Which one of us ever stops to seriously think of what the Lord said: **"For what shall it profit a person if he would gain the whole world, and lose his own soul?"** And: **"What can a person give in exchange for his soul?"** (Matthew 16:26) I ask again, — how many pause to make time to think on this?

The Olympic Games this year were held, as we know, in Sydney Australia. It must never elude us, that these Games, even if greatly embellished and held every four years the world over, are a heritage of Ancient Greece from 776 B.C.

The athletes in ancient Greece were individuals imbued with the highest ideals. They believed that which all athletes should live by: *"A healthy mind in a sound body!"* The athletes were treated with great respect, just as they in turn fully respected their elders. They possessed the sterling quality of ideals, and thus became role models for all, and especially for the youth.

Today, we have top notch athletes in various sports, paid many millions of dollars per year, who get in trouble with the law, oftentimes for serious infractions. How then can these athletes ever serve as role models for our children? But, they surely do!

Should there not be a code, that certain moral standards be upheld by every athlete **without exception,** and when these are violated, their contract would automatically be terminated?

This would be a very powerful lesson for morally borderline athletes, as well as for our youth, who choose them for their role models.

There should be a code of decency, which would prevent these errant athletes from scandalizing the people and especially our youth. But, much to our dismay, athletics in the last couple of decades have become a very lucrative business; so much so, that a decision to dismiss a star athlete for some infraction of the law doesn't even merit discussion! After all, *"money is the name of the game!"*

We have long forgotten, that the healthy standard of athletics and athletes should be, **not who wins, - but how the game is played.**

Our youths idolize the Athletic, Movie and TV celebrities, as well as the Rock stars, and have them as role models. Why? Simply because the true models of character are missing. Consequently, what good can ever be expected from the whole picture facing us today?

In the last days of finishing this book, I happened to have saved a clipping of a column published in the *Daytona Beach Sunday News Journal,* July 16, 2000, which must have appeared in all the Papers of our Nation receiving the news via the Associated Press. It was titled: **"Parental Violence in Sports Escalates."** I quote from the article some of the incidents.

"In Boston, a father who doesn't like a call at his son's Little League game breaks the umpire's jaw." — "A mother at a soccer game slaps a 14 year old referee."

"A police officer thrown out of his son's baseball game later retaliates by pulling the umpire over, and giving him a warning for what he said was an illegal turn."

"Parents have become more invested — perhaps too invested in their children's sports. Some, to the point of violence and vindictiveness. *The recent fatal fist-fight between Fathers at a youth hockey game appears to be an extreme example of a growing trend."*

"I think we saw that one coming. We've seen this behavior escalate and becoming much more violent," says Bob Still, spokesman for a national association of umpires. "It's parents, coaches and players, but mostly parents!"

Another columnist in his article stated: "outbreaks of player and parent violence at kids' sporting events have become part of a bona fide trend." How truly sad!

What a deplorable situation, and what irreparable harm we bring to our children without realizing the impact of our actions. Until I read the above article, I thought we only had *"road rage,"* another meaningless and catastrophic stigma, which is causing the loss of lives needlessly, and bringing a lifetime of grief to suffering innocent families.

Unfortunately, even Leaders in various Churches have submitted to the Pharisaic way of living, -- preaching one thing and in practice doing the opposite.

They resemble those, whom the Lord condemned as **"leaders of the blind!"** (Matthew 15:14; Luke 6:39).

It is also sad, at least from a Christian point of view, to read about some main-line Churches, which until *"yesterday"* held fast to the moral teachings of the Bible, now discussing whether to ordain homosexual men to the Ministry, and to bless same sex unions! I read it in the paper and couldn't believe what I had just read!

Frequently we read of some Minister of a Denomination blessing such unions even though his Church forbids it, and it is positively in contradiction with the Bible.

Still further, while another Denomination does not officially sanction same sex unions and homosexual clergy, yet, this is being practiced within their Denomination to the knowledge of all!

At a recent General Convention, this Denomination's Delegates *"overwhelmingly declared that the Church should* *support unmarried couples — homosexual and heterosexual — in monogamous relationships **honoring religious values!"***

"Honoring religious values!" A profound and edifying declaration indeed, — but how do these Denomination Leaders apply or interpret this? I read this declaration twice, to be sure that I was reading right.

I couldn't believe reading the phrase: ***"honoring religious values!"*** and thought to myself, ***"What honor? What religious values?"*** I am at a loss to comprehend how this Denomination defines ***"honor?"*** Also ***"religious values?"*** We have to wonder, from what *"holy book"* they are drawing their moral teachings, their opinions and practices, because they surely are not from the Holy Bible.

The Holy Scriptures totally and unequivocally condemn what these Delegates are promulgating. Is it any wonder then, why there is such an erosion in our society, and the sliding onto the downhill trend?

So many higher and lower Clergy of the Denominations have forgotten, or have overlooked the purpose of the Church, and have chosen to go with the existing tide!

This is not the case of the Church. The Church has the lofty mission to uplift society, — to uphold the tested values as taught by our Lord, — and not to dance to the rhythm with those, who have renamed and redefined *"sin"* with that word ***"orientation!"*** I would rather they re-label their view as ***"disorientation!"***

Unfortunately, the ranking Clergy of even mainline Denominations are capitulating. My question is, *"why don't the faithful of these Denominations rise up in indignation?"*

Sin has been sugar-coated by those, who should be preaching against immoral acts. Committing immoral acts may not always lead to physical death, but they surely do to spiritual death. St. Paul put it so well when he states: **"The wages of sin is death."** Romans 6:23.

Sadly, we notice the moral fabric of our Nation gradually fraying. The erosion of our Society is almost alarming.

We see the States discussing same sex unions and capitulating. Vermont already passed the law after Hawaii. As the wind blows, we will unfortunately see other States capitulating! The Vermont decision was that of the Lawmakers. However, if the public was asked to vote on the issue you can be sure that this type of a decision would have never passed.

The question is, *"how can we save ourselves from being inundated and drowned by the threatening waters of a dam, which is revealing serious cracks?"*

When I read the newspaper articles pertinent to the above lamentable situations, I blessed myself twice because the Orthodox Church, (perhaps considered antiquated by some, for not following the current trend), stands fast to the moral teachings of the Bible, as interpreted, — **not subjectively, but by the Apostolic and Church Fathers, as well as from the edicts of the local and Ecumenical Councils.**

The Christian Orthodox tradition is consonant with St. Paul's preaching, **"Jesus Christ, the same yesterday, and today, and forever."** Hebrews 13:8.

It follows then, that the Eternal Values **never** change. They are the same **yesterday, today, and forever!**

Society may evolve and rise to unimaginable heights, — progressing materially, scientifically, technologically and intellectually, but if this progress is detached from the verified and proven Eternal Values it will amount to what the Lord had taught in the following verses of Matthew 7:24-25.

*"Therefore, **everyone who hears these words of Mine, and acts upon them,** may be compared to a wise man,*

who built his house upon the rock. And the rain descended, and the floods came, and the winds blew, and burst against that house; and yet it did not fall, for it had been founded upon the rock."

*"And **everyone who hears these words of Mine, and does not act upon them,** will be like a foolish man, who built his house upon the sand. And the rain descended, and the floods came, and the winds blew, and burst against that house; and it fell, and great was its fall."*

We live in the Greatest Country of all, with an over-abundance of the material. Yet, we are spiritual famished. As a result, we are summarily unhappy and surely unfulfilled.

We're living in an age when everybody seems to be in overdrive, without taking the time to analyze why this overhanging cloud of unhappiness exists. Some people recognizing the void that they sense in their life, oftentimes find a quick "fix" to temporarily satisfy themselves with pseudo-cures of the "New Age," "Dianetics," etc. offered to them. They search in every direction, except to the eternal road of fulfillment, as guaranteed by the Lord Himself.

The answer to those seekers, simple as it may seem, is the neglect to learn and believe the guarantee given by the Lord when He said: *"Come unto Me, all you that labor and are heavily laden, and I will give you rest."* Matthew 11:28

It also can be said, that we are living in a highly confused society, where the indecent is supplanting the decent; where disrespect is replacing respect; where gentleness is being replaced with coarseness; where kind words are capitulating to blatant profanities!

There is complete disregard for the Commandments of God. The problem is, that those who break these Commandments know full well, that which they are doing is against God's will, and that they are committing mortal sin.

But they engage significant efforts to *"lullaby"* their conscience, so as to justify their actions by saying: *"everybody's doing it!"* What a lame defense! They forget that in the Last Judgement there will be no "group questioning," but everyone will be judged individually. Therefore, *"everybody's doing it"* will not stand.

I'll never forget a phrase of the late Bishop Fulton Sheen from one of his inspiring, and spiritually productive shows over T.V. in the 50's when he said: **"Right is right, even if one person in the whole world is right; and wrong is wrong, even if the whole world is wrong!"** That is the answer to those who justify their actions by saying: *"everybody's doing it."*

Recently I clipped an item from the ***"Letters to the Editor"*** of a local Newspaper. Among other things, the letter writer stated: *"they've taken melody out of music, beauty out of art, grace out of dancing, and have given nothing worthwhile to take place of what's missing.*

They've given society loud mouths, confrontation, coarseness, dirty language, crassness; and an obsession with sex, materialism and drug abuse. They have amplified guitars and drums, repeat the same three or four words and three or four notes endlessly and call it 'music.' The more weird the blasting sounds and the more repetition, the better they like it. What a sad and unwanted heritage to leave their children!

Let us hope that the remnant of young people who respect family values will stand up one day and say, 'Enough!' We need to return to decency and moderation, which have been neglected for so long!"

We witness rampant unhappiness only because we have substituted the God-given natural law and instincts, with the unnatural. This may be comparable with the traveling on a smoothly paved highway, and suddenly coming onto an endless rocky, bumpy road, which surely punishes the automobile as much as the occupants.

We mentioned *"road rage"* and *"parental rage."* What about *"youth rage?"* Our young people, even from premature ages, are doing things, that only grown people did a generation ago! Now we have guns and shootings in the schools — murders committed by pre-teenagers — metal detectors and regular police in the schools, etc., etc., not to mention the rampant promiscuity, which destroys and perverts these youngsters from their early formative years!

Where will it end? It seems to me that we are using *"band aids"* only, in our attempt to treat the serious wounds of our society!

The Golden Rule, perhaps unknown to many is the solution to Society's ills. *"And as you wish that men would do to you, do so to them."* Luke 6:31.

Draconian measures must be taken if we are ever to fall in line. If we can't discipline ourselves, someone has to do it for us, so that self respect may once again be an adornment to self and society.

Our whole method of operation seems to be upside down. The liberals have succeeded in occupying all the bases. They are proponents of no prayers in the schools — of removing the Ten Commandments, wherever they are posted — of removing the *manger scenes* from the lawns of public buildings, etc. — but these same *"protectors"* of human rights, not even for a moment hesitate to freely espouse the filth and the trash which gushes over TV and the movies, warping so many minds and systematically poisoning the minds and souls of our impressionable children. *THIS IS WRONG!*

Until a generation or so ago, our Constitutional Amendments maintained a proper balance for our expressions. Now, all this *"freedom"* (interpreted: **"license"**) taken from the First Amendment has been seriously misconstrued. It is subjectively and erroneously misinterpreted today, granting in fact a personal *"license"* to interpret and contest situations that arise only for personal benefit.

True freedom is not the right to do as we please, but the opportunity for us to use freedom to do what is right. The freedom to personally interpret the first Amendment, using it as *"license"* gives anyone the right to express himself/herself in any way one desires. By this liberal formula, it follows that people supposedly have the right to use gutter language, even if it is offensive to the majority!

As a result, we have the young tots of Kindergarten and First Grade hurling four letter words at the Teachers, without even knowing what they are really saying. From where do they get this? Where else, but from the home, and the media.

The First Amendment grants the right for free speech and rightfully so. **It is a precious right to be safe-guarded at all costs, but not abused.**

It is a superb guarantee to have the right to express one's opinion on all matters. But, did the Fathers of the Constitution mean, as some loosely interpret, to open the flood gates of sewers and cesspools to contaminate society? Most definitely not. The *"legal twisters"* of today are surely making hay with the First Amendment.

One also wonders why the nine wise Justices of the Supreme Court cannot render decisions based on the Eternal Values on which our Country was founded and made it strong, and which Values the majority of our citizenry espouses even today?

But what happens? One person, being able to escalate from Court to Court and come before the Supreme Court is equal to 250,000,000 Americans, and can turn things upside down, as has been experienced! Can this be right?

Do you remember what a shock it was around our Nation to have heard Clark Gable say in *"Gone with the Wind," "Frankly Ma'm, I don't give a 'damn'! "* This was in 1939 if I recall, and was generally considered blatant profanity. It took years to get over it. But look at what comes over TV and the Movies today! Just think of the filth to which we are exposing to our society and especially to our young people.

It is then natural for our children growing up in this liberal, permissive and very loose environment to perceive that this is the nature of, and the way life really is!

Some expound the opinion, that our young people are in a position of their own, to discern matters of life and make their own decisions about what constitutes life, as it should be lived. But how can this be, when they grow up in a society of moral laxity and permissiveness with no holds barred, and adjust their thinking that this is what constitutes life? This is such a hollow idea.

Little do our young people know that in reality, life is just the opposite of what they hear, see and learn, and that to which they are mostly exposed!

No wonder so many of our young people are confused and founder! On what foundation can they ever build a truly happy life?

Consequently, if society persists on staying on this course, we cannot but reap what we sow. If a way to turn things around is not found, the *"harvest"* of the future, without question, will be deplorable and surely catastrophic!

We could go on and on to remark on these and similar incidents, and to discuss them endlessly. I am confident that what I've stated and more, are very familiar to all of us.

But, something must be done to reverse the current, lest we be swiftly washed over the falls. Thus, at this point we shall stop here to ask: *"Why did She cry?"*

Does not a mother weep, when she sees her child straying from the normal path of the traditional Eternal Values, to follow a path which is contrary to the tested Values, and which as a consequence can only spell doom? How can our *"All-Holy Mother"* but not cry, witnessing what has evolved in our Country and in the world?

Thank God though, for those sterling, genuine souls, — the law abiding, God-fearing people, who bring some balance to Society.

They live by the Eternal Values and believe that Christ is the same yesterday, today and forever! That is why it is so important, as citizens of the greatest Country in the world to accept and shoulder our personal responsibility, to work and help revive the spirit that made our Country great!

Each one of us must submit ourselves to self-discipline and become alert by opening up the eyes and ears of our heart, to recognize the God-sent *Manifestations*.

These *"Signs"* are nothing short of *"wake-up calls,"* for the many who are straddling the moral fence to their detriment.

Our *"All-Holy Mother, the Ever Virgin Mary,"* our most deeply revered Mother wept openly, — to touch our hearts, so that we would conscientiously endeavor to find our way back to the path of peace, respect, kindness, empathy, contentment and brotherly love, which are the veritable guarantees for happiness, so universally desired.

In brief, I believe that our *"All-Holy Mother"* shed tears seeing our spiritual and moral laxity. She wept and weeps for the apostasy of our modern people from the Truth.

How well it would be to analyze our moral and spiritual predicament, instead of analyzing the tears! The tears are there, not to be analyzed and defined by a laboratory, but to arouse us to introspection and self-examination. They are not simply to be marveled at, but to make us shed our own tears in repentance — and enable us to find the road back.

"Why did She cry?" **My hope, and my prayer is, — that She didn't cry — as many mothers have, — in vain!**

Glossary

Akathist Hymn — (The accent is on the capital **A**).
Akathist means *"not seated."* The initial Service in 626 A.D. was prayed with everyone standing,

Apse — The semi-circular part of a building, especially in a Church having a concave surface.

Iconostasis — (I-con-**OS**-ta-sis).
The screen, or wall separating the Sanctuary from the Nave is seen in all Orthodox Churches. On this decorative separation the Icons are placed.
— Also, the corner in a room of an Orthodox home where the Icons are hung for Family worship. In this Book, the home *"Iconostasis"* is referred to as *"The Family Altar."*

Narthex — We enter the Church through the *"Narthex"* (vestibule) which brings us into the Nave. In the Ancient Church only the Baptized Christians were permitted to follow the Divine Liturgy in the Nave.
— The *"Catechumens,"* were candidates being instructed in preparation for their Baptism.They followed the first part of the Liturgy in the Nave, that is, until after the reading of the Gospel followed by the Sermon, and then would be dismissed to the Narthex.
— Also, Christians who had fallen into mortal sin, did part of their penance by being remanded to the Narthex. After Confession and absolution, they could re-enter into the Nave to participate in the Liturgy.

Nave — From the Greek word **"Naus,"**(Nufs) meaning "ship." It is the root of the words "Navy, nautical," etc.
The Congregation follows the Services in the Nave. Symbolically, the Congregation is in the **"Ship,"** carrying its passengers to the port of salvation.

Hodegetria — ("O-the-**YEE**-tree-uh.)"

> *"Hodegetria"* literally means, *"the one who directs, or shows the way."* This was the title of the Icon of the All-Holy Mother, traditionally painted by St. Luke the Evangelist.

Orea Pili — ("Oh-**REH**-uh **PEE**-lee)."

> The entrance way of the Icon Screen from the Nave to the Sanctuary. Literally in Greek, it means *"Beautiful Portal or Gate."*

Panagia — ("Pun-uh-**YEE**-uh.)"

> A synthetic Greek word (Pan-agia), meaning *"All-Holy."* In Greek, when we refer to the *"All-Holy Mother"*, we usually say *"Panagia."*

Pantocrator — (pun-toe-**CRUT**-tor).

> It is a synthetic word. "Panto-crator" means, *"holding all in His hands"* (referring to God). The Lord Jesus is painted inside the dome of the Orthodox Churches. This portrayal is labeled *"Pantocrator.)"*

Paraklesis — ("Puh-**RUH**-klee-sis.)"

> A special Service of petition to the *"Panagia."*

Pendentives — The triangular surfaces below the dome, which are automatic ally formed when the arches in the vaulted ceilings of the Nave meet in the corners, supported by four columns. Usually in the pendentives we see the Icons of the four Evangelists.

Platytera — ("Plut tee-**TERR**-uh).)"

> Alludes to the *"All Holy Mother,"* the *"Panagia."* She is portrayed in the apse of the Sanctuary in the Orthodox Churches with Her arms widely outstretched. She is described as *"Broader than the*

Heavens" (in Greek: *"Platytera)"* and referred to as such, in one of the hymns of the Divine Liturgy.

Portaitissa — ("Port-uh- **EE**-tee-suh.)"

The name or title, given to the Icon of the second Manifestation. The original is in the Monastery of Iveron on Mt. Athos in Greece. Literally, it means *"Mother of the Portals,* or *Gate."*

Royal Doors, or Gates — These are the doors in the center of the *"Iconostasis"* at the *"Orea Pili"* which remain closed when there are no Services.

Sanctuary — The area behind the Icon Screen or Wall. In the Sanctuary, we see the Holy Altar in the center, and the *"Prothesis"* to the left, (preparation Table for the Holy Gifts to be offered in the Divine Liturgy).
Only the Clergy and the Altar Boys, who have been tonsured by the Bishop enter the Sanctuary.

Theotokos — ("Theh-oh-**TOE**-kose.)"

Literally meaning, the *"Birth-Giver of God."* It is a synthetic Greek word (Theo-tokos); the Virgin Mary, who gave birth to the Lord Jesus ' human counterpart.

Transepts — The right and left wings, or extensions of the Nave, which together with the Nave and the Sanctuary form a cross, the traditional shape of the Orthodox Church edifice. At the crosspiece of the Nave, we look up at the Dome to see the Icon of the Pantocrator.

✳